PARENT-TEACHER CONFERENCING

Gerda Lawrence, M.S.W.

Madeline Hunter, Ed.D.

TIP Publications

El Segundo, California

i

THEORY INTO PRACTICE PUBLICATIONS

Motivation Theory for Teachers
Reinforcement Theory for Teachers
Retention Theory for Teachers
Teach More—Faster!
Teach for Transfer
Prescription for Improved Instruction
Aide-ing in Education
Improving Your Child's Behavior

Copyright 1978, Gerda Lawrence and Madeline Hunter
TIP Publications
P.O. Box 514
El Segundo, California 90245

First Printing, August, 1978
Second Printing, December, 1980
Third Printing, May, 1982
Fourth Printing, November, 1983
Fifth Printing, December, 1984
Sixth Printing, August, 1985
Seventh Printing, April 1, 1986

PRINTED IN THE UNITED STATES OF AMERICA

FOREWORD

The purpose of this book is to help you conduct conferences that are satisfying to you and to parents.

To accomplish this, we will discuss setting reasonable objectives for your conferences, the professional skills that will help you to achieve these objectives, how to evaluate success, and some things to do when you find that you were not as successful as you had hoped.

We will describe techniques that can help you plan for your conferences, ways to conduct them more skillfully, and how to "build bridges" for follow-up work.

You will find suggestions for ways to say things so that the chances of being understood are increased, how to say difficult things without the kind of pain that often blocks communication, how to obtain information useful to you in working more effectively with your students, and how to encourage parents to work with you to further students' learning.

We will discuss pitfalls in conferencing and deal with some thorny problems, such as how to respond to angry, verbally abusive parents, and ways you can reach out to seemingly unavailable or reluctant parents.

This book will not tell you *what* the content of your conferences should be and *which* conference objectives are most appropriate. Reading this book, however, should help you base your decisions on theories and techniques developed by experts in communication so you will more likely achieve the objectives you and the parent have set.

The examples in this book are taken from the authors' own experiences in educational communication; while the focus is on parent conferencing, the technical and theoretical information discussed is applicable to other human communication. Consequently, the ideas presented will contribute not only to better parent conferencing, but also to more effective teacher-student conferencing, principal-teacher conferencing, smoother interaction of school faculties, and more successful communication between educators and lay citizens as they jointly participate in parent-teacher and advisory groups.

Let us know how well we have communicated with you.

Gerda Lawrence
Madeline Hunter

"THE FRONT OFFICE"

Some of the most important and effective home-school communication is accomplished by the "front office" staff of secretaries, clerks and volunteers as they respond to parents' requests for information, help in finding a lost sweater or lunch box, assistance with a child who is ill or a sympathetic person with whom to register a complaint.

These "mini conferences" often constitute the introduction to a school when the child is enrolled, provide the maintenance of day to day communication and the avenue through which a parent indicates dissatisfaction.

The authors wish to express personal appreciation to the gracious and skilled front office staff at the University Elementary School at UCLA. The following people serve as models for all school staffs because they not only are enabling to parents, but make our professional work possible.

Margaret Devers
Leona Disosway
Kate Lubbin
Lillian Ostroff
Pat Pate
Nancy Shilling
Kay Wallace

To
Edith, David and Annette
and
to the staff and parents of the
University Elementary School
University of California, Los Angeles
who have taught, inspired, supported
and believed in us,
this book is affectionately and respectfully dedicated.

Gerda Lawrence

Madeline Hunter

CONTENTS

INTRODUCTION
Why Have Parent-Teacher Conferences?.   1

Section I   TYPES OF CONFERENCES
 1. THE GROUP CONFERENCE
    How do I introduce parents to my program?   6
 2. THE REPORTING CONFERENCE
    How is the student doing?   8
 3. THE INFORMATION-GETTING CONFERENCE
    Can you tell me about....?   15
 4. THE PROBLEM-SOLVING CONFERENCE
    What shall we do about....?   19

Section II   CONFERENCING SKILLS
 5. REASONABLE EXPECTATIONS
    What can be accomplished in one conference?   25
 6. ESTABLISHING THE CONFERENCE OBJECTIVE
    Are we agreed on our focus?   27
 7. PREPARATION FOR CONFERENCES
    What do I do to get ready?   31
 8. OPENING STATEMENTS
    How do I start?   33
 9. FORMULATING THE MESSAGE
    How do I say it?   34
10. THE CHECK-BACK
    What did you hear?   42
11. CLOSING THE CONFERENCE
    How do I end?   44
12. JUDGING THE SUCCESS OF A CONFERENCE
    How did it go?   46

Section III   COMMUNICATION THEORY
13. COMMUNICATION
    Will theory help?   49
14. EMOTIONS AFFECT COMMUNICATION
    Watch out—it's hot!   51
15. VALUES AFFECT COMMUNICATION
    Watch out—it's loaded!   55

Section IV   SPECIAL CONSIDERATIONS

16. AUGMENTING THE CONFERENCE WITH ADDITIONAL PARTICIPANTS
    Who should be present? 61
17. THE STUDENT'S ROLE IN PARENT CONFERENCES
    What are students' rights and responsibilities? 63
18. THE TELEPHONE CONFERENCE
    Is this a good time to talk?. 65
19. CONFIDENTIALITY
    With whom may I share information? 71

Section V   SPECIAL PROBLEMS

20. BEING THE BEARER OF BAD TIDINGS
    How do I communicate unwelcome information? 77
21. A LISTENING POST FOR PARENTS
    To be or not to be? 80
22. ADVICE-SEEKING PARENTS
    Should I tell them what to do? 81
23. RELUCTANT PARENTS
    How do I get them to a conference?. 83
24. THE ANGRY, VERBALLY ABUSIVE PARENT
    What do I do when they are mad?. 85
25. THE UNSCHEDULED, "DROP IN" CONFERENCE
    Do you have a minute?. 87
26. PREMATURE CLOSURES
    Let's settle it quickly 90

Section VI   LOGISTICS

27. THE TIME, THE PLACE AND THE SETTING
    Where and when?. 92

Section VII   SAMPLE FORMS ....

Invitation to Group Conference 96
Invitation to Reporting Conference 97
Written Summaries 98
Follow-up Letters 100
Weekly Note 102
Student Questionnaires 103

INTRODUCTION

Dear Parents:

Our school's cross-graded, multiethnic, individualized learning program is designed to enhance the concept of an open-ended learning program with emphasis on a continuum of multiethnic academically enriched learning, using the identified intellectually gifted child as the agent or director of his own learning.

Major emphasis is on cross-graded, multiethnic learning with the main objective being to learn respect for the uniqueness of a person.

Signed _____
Principal

When this message was received by the parent of a high school pupil, he sent the following response:

Dear Principal:

I have a college degree, speak two foreign languages and four Indian dialects, have been to a number of county fairs and three goat ropings, but I haven't the faintest idea as to what the hell you are talking about. Do you?

Signed "A Bewildered Parent"

"What *are* you talking about?" is not the response to a communication transmitted in an unknown language, but a cry of distress when a message conveyed in a known language is not understood. It is to reduce such distress and increase the chances for effective communication between home and school that this book has been written.

Parents and teachers are inextricably joined in one of the most important human enterprises because they share the major responsibility for the education and socialization of youth. Therefore, communication with parents is an important adjunct to the teacher's main business—teaching students.

Parent conferences, initiated by schools, have increased markedly in recent years. In the past, a parent-teacher conference that did not deal with a problem ("I'm going to have to see your parents") often was informal or happenstance at PTA meetings, in the hall, or at the grocery store. Now, more and more school districts are designating the parent conference as the official report of student progress.

The effort to achieve more meaningful communication about student progress evolved because the formal procedure of a report card or checklist could do little more than label categories in which a student was placed ("doing well," "needs to improve"), or convey a terse message by a phrase or comment. No longer is this satisfying to teacher or parent. Students who occupy the same category of an "A" or a "C" can be very different indeed. That difference can be meaningfully conveyed only by skillful reporting in teacher-parent communication.

In addition to academic information, parents need to know (and the school wants them to know) how their child makes and keeps friends, relates to adults, fares under stress, bounces back from adversity, approaches new tasks, and presents him/herself to the world. This kind of information is best conveyed when parents and teachers talk together.

Other conferences are requested by teachers because they need information to gain a clearer understanding of the student in order to design a more effective learning environment.

Conferences are also requested for educational problems which can most easily be ameliorated when parent help is engaged and a cooperative home-school plan is developed. Through conferences, school and home can become a problem solving team with high potential for success. An example of a problem which responds to this unanimity of environmental support is the situation when a student feels that home and school have different values and/or varying expectations for performance.

Additionally, the parent conference provides a way to extend parenting skills. Teachers can assist parents in learning how to help the child acquire a new behavior, additional knowledge, increased skills or to practice new learnings outside of school. For example, it may be easier for the parent to demonstrate that mathematical relationships exist in everyday activities. Computation can be made more meaningful by counting the number of pieces of silverware needed to set the table, the change due at a store, the minutes left to play outdoors, or by measuring baking ingredients or lumber. Being responsible for making a shopping list and then selecting the items at the store makes reading, writing and arithmetic practical assets.

Learning gains from out-of-school practice can range from increased motor coordination to complex reading or thinking if the parents have achieved the skills necessary for extending their child's thinking and encouraging effective practice. Enrichment from the fine arts can be realized by the actions of parents. In short, if parents are encouraged and assisted to become engaged in a collaborative educational effort, parenting can become a powerful adjunct to the program of the school as well as effectively instill the concerns, values and expectations of the home: a worthy outcome of parent conferencing.

Not only are teachers seeking more contacts with parents, parents feel more comfortable asking teachers to meet with them. Many parents seek information which only the teacher, who works in a group learning situation with the child, possesses. To many parents, the teacher is the most knowledgeable professional available with whom to talk about the daily functioning of their child: how (s)he learns, the success of his/her relationships with adults and children outside the home, and how (s)he measures up to others the same age. The teacher, as the source of this kind of information, has become important because today's families are smaller and often without close ties to relatives or long intimate associations with friends. The information and support supplied in the past by relatives, the family physician, and religious institutions is less available to many parents.

Parents also turn to teachers as knowledgeable professionals for help with problems of child raising, with requests ranging from appropriate reading materials for the child, to how to get him/her to practice music, go to bed on time, or make and hold friends.

Teachers and parents talking together about concerns vital to both, the growth and development of the child, has become such a common activity that one wonders why it should require special thinking, planning and writing about. By the time people become adults, shouldn't their communication be quite effective and satisfying? Much of the time, yes. But when we inspect many things we do habitually, we often find they are not done as well as they could be and, as a result, do not yield satisfaction to the parties involved.

Many teachers have shared with us their distress about the inadequacy of their preparation and the lack of useful written material for conferencing with parents. Many parents have told us of their wish for "getting more out of conferences with my child's teacher."

In preservice education, most teachers have had little or no training for the sensitive task of conducting a productive conference, nor is there adequate inservice help. Consequently, success, or lack of it, often is dependent on intuitive abilities and hit and miss learning from mistakes, rather than on systematic acquisition of conferencing skills. Yet, teachers know that their professional skill in working with parents, just as in teaching students, is a critical variable that determines what will be accomplished.

Luckily, some conferences are relatively simple to conduct (after all, we do have successful students, marvelous parents, and talented, accomplished teachers). Many conferences, however, take place under emotionally stressful conditions and can have far reaching consequences for student success, parents' feelings about schools, public support of education, and teachers' professional satisfaction. The skill to formulate and convey a clear and cogent message to the parent is critical. Equally critical are the skills to help the parent understand information about his/her child, to elicit from the parent information about the child which is useful to the teacher, or to assist the parent to help with solving an educational problem the student encounters, or acquire a parenting skill which could result in improved student functioning.

Successful and satisfying communication in parent conferences builds a foundation of trust. Knowing that their children are progressing well or, if they aren't, that something constructive is being done to improve the situation, generates parents' faith in the integrity of school personnel. As a result, parents are more willing to listen to, seriously consider, respect and support the professional point of view. These bonds of trust and respect between educators, parents, and citizens are so important that satisfactory communication should not be left to chance, but serious effort needs to be expended in its development.

An additional dividend from satisfying and productive parent conferences is the transfer of the knowledge and skills learned to parent volunteers or advisory groups. Parents need criteria for judging which educational goals are realistic, and the professional skills required to make those goals attainable. Through conferencing with teachers, parents can learn to appreciate the critical importance of a highly competent professional staff augmented by supporting parent groups in order to achieve goals of accountability.

Effective communication has emerged as a critical attribute of success in both parent conferences and work with volunteers and lay advisory groups. Needless to say, however, *no amount of effective communication can ameliorate the effects of an inadequate program. The quality of the educational program is the basic foundation on which satisfactory and successful communication is built.*

In summary, productive communication achieved in parent conferences fulfills parents' and teachers' needs for sharing information, for working together to augment students' success and diminish problems and for enhancing those skills which increase productive collaboration.

Section I   TYPES OF CONFERENCES

1. THE GROUP CONFERENCE
   How do I introduce my program? 6

2. THE REPORTING CONFERENCE
   How is the student doing? 8

3. THE INFORMATION-GETTING CONFERENCE
   Can you tell me about....? 15

4. THE PROBLEM-SOLVING CONFERENCE
   What shall we do about....? 19

THE GROUP CONFERENCE

"Tutoring is wasteful when individuals could learn just as well in a group," applies not only to classroom teaching but to parent conferencing as well. Consequently, at the beginning of the school year, a group parent meeting serves as a general get-acquainted, information-giving conference. Much time can be saved in subsequent individual conferences, because:

1. Parents have had a chance to become acquainted with their child's teacher and know what (s)he is like.

2. They have seen the classroom, materials and books and have heard what their child will study and be expected to accomplish in school and through homework.

3. They have learned some ways they can assist in that accomplishment and what to do if there is a problem.

4. They have been informed about how and when they will receive more specific information about their child.

5. They have had general first-of-the-year concerns and questions answered.

The invitation to the group conference must stress that individual children or specific situations will *not* be discussed (see *Sample Invitation*, page 96). During the meeting, we must remain courteously adamant in refusing to respond to the normal and inevitable "How is my child doing?" overtures of some parents. A warm but firm, "I want to talk about that too, but today's/tonight's not the time. Let's make an appointment," usually works.

SAMPLE AGENDA FOR A GROUP PARENT MEETING.

The times suggested reflect approximations, not a prescribed number of minutes.

7:30—*Getting acquainted.*
Parent name tags, with child's name also, should be available. Students can make and decorate these name tags as a classroom project before the conference or parents can make them as they arrive.

Coffee at the beginning is a useful "time blotter" which enables us to circulate, parents to become acquainted, and accommodates the inevitable late arrivals.

7:45—*Objectives for the year.*

The presentation phase of the meeting begins with a statement of general objectives for the year. These objectives need to be described in terms of specific content to be learned (i.e. report writing, U.S. History, division, etc.), with examples of acceptable products in each area (a page of math, samples of creative writing, crafts, criteria for a research report). Objectives should include social, physical and aesthetic as well as academic areas of growth. The presentation phase should answer most of the questions the parents sent in on the response section of the invitation.

8:15—*How parents can contribute to students' achievement.*

We need to give examples of parent assistance which are appropiate for all students, such as:

"Provide a half hour of reading time each evening when T.V. is turned off."

"Make up rhyming words, synonyms, definitions, etc., when riding in a car."

"Check child's number facts occasionally, or when you receive a note to do so."

"Take your child to the library at a specified time each week."

We also need to assure parents that the specific homework needs of each student will be dealt with at individual conferences or by phone communication.

Information about scheduling regular parent conferences, how students will be involved in those conferences, how parents may reach the teacher if there is a concern, and assurance that the teacher will call the parents should a need arise, will set ground rules for future communication.

8:30—*Response to parent questions.*

We respond to the queries of parents that were obtained through the invitation questionnaire and not covered in the presentation. Those questions must be screened as to their relevance to the total group. The of-interest-to-only-one questions should be answered individually at an agreed upon time and not imposed on the group.

Additional questions may be accepted from the group (if deemed appropriate) or we can indicate we'll remain a few minutes after the meeting to answer additional questions.

8:45—*Expression of appreciation for parents' attendance and prompt dismissal.*

Parents are tired. We are tired and we don't let the meeting drag on past the specified time. If coffee is served after the meeting, we are prepared with a technique for clearing the house: "Five more minutes before it's time to go home so tomorrow our children have rested parents and teachers."

A successful group conference sets the tone for the year and builds anticipation of satisfying future home-school communication.

THE REPORTING CONFERENCE

Parents have the right to and responsibility for periodically securing information about their child's functioning in school. Our responsibility is to report to parents *what* and *how well* their youngster has learned during a specified time period. The reporting conference accommodates those rights and fulfills those responsibilities.

Describing a student's performance meaningfully and accurately is the cornerstone of all effective conferencing. We need to convey what and how well a child is doing through meaningful words and significant examples of classroom work so that parents can "see" their child's performance at school. Matched mind pictures ("I see what you mean") are critical to the communicative process. (See *Chapter 13*)

Successful reporting depends to a large extent on:

1. Adequate preparation on the part of the teacher; thinking through what is significant about *this* student and how best to convey that information. *Chapter 7* describes preparation for a reporting conference.

2. Use of clear, concise, enabling language with enough information so the parent "gets the picture" without being overwhelmed by unncessary words or too many examples. *Chapter 9* deals with ways to formulate the report so that parents participate in the communicative interaction.

3. Selection, with the parent, of what aspects of student performance to highlight in the conference. Should focus be on one or two areas of particular significance or concern, with other aspects of student functioning only briefly covered? Or should there be fairly even distribution of time on all major aspects?

In many conferences, parents or teachers have special interests or concerns. It is, therefore, important to determine through a questionnaire prior to the conference (see *appendix*, page 97 for sample) or to open the conference with an inquiry: "Is there an area in which you have particular interest? If so, we'll start with that." Or, "Even though I am ready to talk about all of Raul's subjects, I would like to start with how he is making and keeping friends, because that has been so very important to him this year." Or, "You've noted on the questionnaire that you want to spend some time today talking about how Joanna feels about herself since she often seems scared when she has to tackle something new." *Chapter 6* further discusses the importance of jointly establishing a conference objective.

Parents who regularly see their child's work or who often check informally with the teacher, do not need to be told in detail about every aspect of the curriculum. A justifiable criticism of some reporting conferences is that parents are told things they already know. We can eliminate this by beginning with a summary of what the parent already knows and then moving to new information. For example, "You are aware of how well Maria is doing in reading and math. So, if it's O.K. with you, I'll start with her writing skills. I don't think you've seen what she has done most recently."

Parents who have not seen their child's work or have not talked with the teacher, need a more comprehensive progress report which includes the description of what the student has studied or accomplished in: academic subjects, social interactions, emotional development, physical (large and small muscle) skills, and classroom behavior.

Academic Performance

Most parents are concerned about their child's learning in reading, writing and arithmetic. It is our job to give information of progress in basic skills and, if there is a problem, what is being done about it. We also need to report the child's performance in other subjects such as social studies, the arts, and education. Examples:

"Bill now reads in the 3rd preprimer. He knows the words and understands what he reads. This is his current book."

"Felicia is in an independent reading program. That means she can choose many different books. Right now she likes adventure stories."

"David has just started division problems such as _____."

"Annette is in a group working on Haiku poetry which she really enjoys. Here are some of the poems she has written."

"In our study of nutrition we have identified how each food group is important to our health. Eric has seemed really interested. Has he told you about some of the foods we have prepared?"

"I want to show you some of the art work Hal has done. He has a lovely sense of color and form. Art is one of the subjects he really enjoys."

"In music, Robby is developing an excellent singing voice and a fine sense of rhythm. Has he sung some of the songs he's learned?"

Social Development

It is important for parents to know how their youngster works and plays with classmates, relates to adults and functions as a member of a larger group.

"Manuel works well with others and often is chosen as a partner."

"May sometimes put down others with a comment such as, 'That's a dumb answer,' or 'Mine is better.' We need to help her learn to be more tolerant of others."

"It is hard for Maury to throw or catch a ball as well as most boys in the class. That makes it difficult for him to be part of the group with which he would like to play."

"Harry works well with a small group of friends, but still doesn't volunteer his good ideas or speak out in a larger group."

Emotional Development

It is also important that we tell parents how we see their child's emotional development. How does (s)he approach new tasks, bounce back from adversity, fare under stress, react to frustration, see her/himself as a growing person in a world which often presents challenges and which includes both successes and failures? Examples:

"Benny hasn't yet learned that his work is O.K. He seems to feel if he does something, it's sure to be wrong, and if he's right, it's an accident."

"Betty says she 'doesn't care' but her expression is that of a very disappointed little girl."

"It's not that Larry is not doing well. It's that he still gets discouraged so easily if he feels something is not perfect."

"Charlotte is a bouncy girl. Even when she doesn't easily succeed in something, she says, 'O.K., I'll try it again' and off she goes."

"Leonard always has excellent ideas. Now he takes the time to write them down. His face shows that he is very pleased with himself."

"Eva hasn't yet learned to distinguish between intentional and accidental slights or hurts. A stray ball that hits her or a child who brushes against her upsets her as much as if someone went out of the way to strike her."

Physical Development

Descriptions of the student's ability to use his/her body in work, play and as a medium of expression are an important part of the reporting conference. Examples:

"Doris has good coordination and is a fast runner. Now she is working on throwing and catching. She is trying hard and her skills are improving."

"Bill is growing fast and that may be the reason he finds physical activities difficult. It is understandable that he tries to avoid games that require a high degree of skill."

"Helen's small muscle skills are coming along. We have been giving her a lot of practice in cutting, pasting, working with puzzles and small objects like Lego."

"Edith is now spacing her letters evenly. Here is one of her papers."

Classroom Behavior

Next to concern about academic performance, most parents want to know how their child "behaves" at school. Examples:

"Beryl is a very considerate youngster. Her good manners are a credit to you."

"Danielle is still so eager to be heard she blurts out answers. This makes things difficult for her and others."

"Aaron can always be counted on to do his best work."

"Donald hasn't yet learned to stay in his seat when it's quiet work time. He and I have worked out a plan that should help."

In addition to knowing *what* their child is doing, parents need to know *how* the teacher evaluates their child's performance and behavior. Is it something to be proud of, concerned about, typical of that age, a sign of growth for the student, no cause to worry? To answer the question, "How is my child doing?" with integrity requires professional judgement based on observation of student products and behaviors over a period of time. Such judgements are a part of our professional responsibility.

Positive information is usually welcome and, therefore, easy for parents to hear and for us to state. Not-so-positive information may be hard for parents to hear and is often difficult for us to state. Therefore, it is important we not get lured into the trap of minimizing that not-so-welcome information, leaving it to the end of the conference when not enough time is available for it or, in an effort to dilute it, stating it unclearly. The difficulty we often have in being the bearer of bad tidings is discussed further in *Chapter 20*.

Sometimes the significance of how the student is doing is implied by what (s)he does. After all, if Bill is in the first grade and reading at a third level, he's doing well indeed; if Paula is expressing a lot of worry about her work, there is some reason for concern about how comfortable she is with herself emotionally. In less obvious situations, we need to select a way to help parents understand the significance of what the student is doing.

Four ways to communicate our professional judgements are descriptions which tell: 1) what a particular student is doing in comparison with other students of the same age. 2) the student's growth or lack of growth during a particular time period. 3) the student's strengths and weaknesses. 4) the student's response to special help on the part of the teacher or the school.

1. *Performance Compared to Age Groups.*

When a student's performance becomes significant because it differs markedly from that of other youngsters of the same age—from a norm—concern or lack of it can best be conveyed through comparison with others. For example, an older youngster may be seen as deficient in mastering the fine motor skills required for letter formation, while a younger child, whose letters also look like hen tracks, is seen as fairly normal in fine motor development. Reading on a preprimer level is normal for a six year old, but a matter of concern when the student is nine years old. Examples:

"Not only is Alice an excellent reader in our class, she is a good year ahead of others her age on a district-wide test."

"In math, Jack performs as expected for his age, both in our class and on a standardized test."

"Cheryl is having a really hard time with fine motor control, more so than most youngsters her age. It shows in her writing."

"Sam hits before he finds out what the problem is. This is typical of younger children, but not for a boy his age."

"Mike has not yet learned how to let other youngsters know he wants to play or work with them. He'll hit or tease, which most boys his age have outgrown."

"Esther always is first to volunteer whenever help is needed. She's unusually aware for a child so young."

"Sharon needs my immediate attention more often than anyone else in the room. Most youngsters her age have learned to wait awhile to have a piece of work checked or a question answered."

A sensitive dilemma exists when the student is apparently learning to the best of his/her ability, but is not on a par with what is typically expected of this age level. Both items of information need to be conveyed clearly to forestall bewilderment later. "You said (s)he was doing fine, but (s)he isn't if (s)he's still not up to where the other kids are." In these cases, the teacher needs to reassure the parents about their child's sincere effort and measureable growth, especially if the parents are inclined to worry or apply more pressure than the child can handle. "You need to know that Bill is working as hard as he can and is making steady growth, but writing is difficult for him and he still is not able to finish his work in the same time as the others."

One more caution: Ever since an alert parent who was told his daughter was "able to do long division now" replied, "O.K., so she is able to, but does she do it?" we have become sensitized to the word *able*, which often is used to mean "(s)he does it." Consequently, we are explicit when a student is *able to* do something but for some reason does not. "Maxine is able to write very neatly. Most of the time, however, even when told to do her best work, she writes hurriedly and far from neatly."

2. *Growth Within a Period.*

The significance of performance often is best conveyed by pointing out that it indicates growth or lack of it. Examples:

"In September, Jonathan, like lots of beginning readers, had forgotten many of the words he had learned. That is typical and it didn't take him long to get back to where he had left off last June. Now he is moving along at a good rate and is reading like most of the youngsters his age."

"Suddenly, Jane caught onto math and is doing fine. It's as if a curtain opened."

"Sally needs to work hard on forming her letters evenly and making them smaller. It's still difficult for her but we can see steady improvement."

"At the beginning of the year, Mary would cry when she was disappointed. Now she asserts her rights when she feels hurt. That is great growth."

"Maria is developing well socially. At the beginning of the year she only watched the other children. Then she began to play alongside them. Now she plays with a few friends. Each month I see her taking another step forward."

"Bill now completes his work even when he's sitting near his friends."

"I don't see the progress we've hoped for in Sally's settling down to work. She still wanders around the room and reacts to everything."

3. Strengths and Weaknesses.

Some youngsters perform superbly in one area (perhaps in reading, sports, or expressing themselves orally), are so-so in other areas (perhaps in computing, or fine motor skills), and are deficient in some areas (perhaps in getting ideas down on paper or social skills). Examples:

"Lynn is a strong reader. Math is much harder for her."

"Judy's mind races ahead of her hand, so she still finds it difficult to get her ideas down on paper."

"In all academic areas, Regina moves rapidly. She thinks well, has excellent ideas, and expresses them easily. Now we are working to help her accept that she doesn't always have to be the first one with the answer, that other people also have ideas and a right to express them, and that she'll learn many things from listening."

4. Response to Special Help.

The student's response to special help, or the effort it takes to make learning possible, may be critical for understanding performance.

Sometimes, this involves determining how the student learns best. What is his/her preferred learning style? Does (s)he need every step carefully explained and monitored with frequent reassurance? Should the teacher carefully "spoon feed" every step of the way with explanations and support? Or, does the student learn best when given his/her head and run with the materials? Does competition, or "bet you can't do it" spur effort? Examples:

"Harry loves to read. My job is to have enough challenging reading material so he finds interesting books on his reading level. Otherwise, he's completely independent."

"I have to work to see that Lynn does her assignments. If I leave her alone, she'll look around, wander, talk with neighbors. I check on her and require that she check with me all through the day. Since I've become that persistent, she has made learning gains."

"Rarely have I seen a youngster work as hard and as patiently as Nancy. Things don't come easily for her, but she always perseveres. You should be proud of her."

"As you know, Marion has a hard time remembering words in reading. We have given her extra help so, with lots of hard work on her and our part, she is doing much better. I'm encouraged, because there is a real spurt in her growth."

13

"Jeanette likes to be a leader. It's still hard for her to follow the ideas of others. At times, she gets quite angry when they don't want to go along with what she wants to do. I have started to use role playing where youngsters take parts in skits and situations based on classroom problems. In that way, Jeanette and others, who also need to learn smoother ways of getting along, have practice in learning social skills by trying out different ways of behaving. I know she likes being in the skits and I believe that kind of practice will be useful to her."

"Paul and I designed a card on which I make a mark every time he's out of his seat and wandering around the room. We are trying to help him get fewer marks each week. For every five marks less than he had the week before, he gets extra choice time. He's responding excellently. Last week he got only eight marks. When he started he would get as many as 40."

In addition to reporting and interpreting student's performance, we also need to communicate *what is being done at school* to *increase* academic, aesthetic, social, emotional and physical growth or *remediate* lack of it, as well as to challenge gifted learners.

Closing the Conference

A satisfying closure of the conference (see *Chapter 11*) includes:

1) A brief summary of main points which wraps up what has been said so the parent can "take it home."

If it is not the school's practice to give parents a written progress report, it is useful to write down, with the parent's help, a very brief summary of main ideas expressed and recommendations made with a carbon retained for the school file. If we do not summarize the main points of the conference in writing *with* the parent, it is well to do so immediately after the conference so agreements are remembered and kept.

2) The decision as to the next contact between school and home. Will it be in a few days or weeks or at the next regularly scheduled meeting time; by phone, notes or in person?

3) The decision as to who will report to a student who was not present in the conference and what information will be reported. (See *Chapter 17*)

Parents should leave a reporting conference with the assurance that the teacher is aware of their interests and concerns, with documented knowledge of how their child is performing and what is being done to enhance that performance in academic and nonacademic areas, and with the feeling that they, as parents, are a valued and contributing part of their child's education.

Can you tell me about. . . . ?

THE INFORMATION GETTING CONFERENCE

Securing information that will facilitate delivery of optimal professional service is a responsibility that education shares with other professions such as law and medicine.

A great deal that affects students' learning happens outside the teacher's span of control. Some of these events have already happened and others will happen at home and in the community. Supports and stresses outside of school influence how a student feels physically, emotionally and socially when (s)he arrives at school each day. Those feelings are reflected in learning success and "making it" in the school world. Therefore, pertinent outside information is indispensable to teachers in order that they, 1) *work* as effectively as possible *in* school and, 2) *evaluate* the effectiveness of that work in the student's life *outside* of school.

EDUCATIONALLY USEFUL INFORMATION
1. *For Designing the School Program*
Teachers need to develop discrimination that detects useful information and culls out information, no matter how fascinating and provocative, which is not useful in teaching the student. The critical question is: What constitutes *useful* information?

Information is useful only when that information helps a teacher work with a particular student, at a particular time. This seemingly obvious statement is the critical discriminator that helps us distinguish between non-useful information (such as irrelevant personal data, excuse making or gossip) and information which is useful in understanding a student better and planning a school program in which that student will be successful.

Whether information is solicited or unsolicited, the guideline is, "Does what I'm hearing help me, (a) work more productively because I have a clearer understanding of the student? or, (b) evaluate better the effectiveness of my teaching?" If the answer to either question is "no," precious conference time should not be wasted on that information.

It can be useful to know a student's outside interests (Dixieland jazz, butterflies, making models, a new telescope) so those interests can be furthered or used as educational springboards to additional learning.

It can be useful to know that Maurice has a new baby brother or sister and, as a result, doesn't have his mind on school but wonders what is going on at home. That does not excuse him from being (or us from letting him be) unproductive. The information, however, may alter our approach so Maurice does not get the impression that his present preoccupation appears unreasonable. Instead we convey to him that his temporary lack of focus is understandable.

It is useful to learn from Lisa's parents that she is less resistive to trying something new if she can practice first in private to lessen the risk of failure in front of others. By knowing this, we can arrange to "prime" Lisa before exposing her to a new situation.

For a student who copes with praise by becoming silly and self-conscious, it is useful to learn that the mother has few child-rearing skills other than punishing for misbehavior. This information suggests we praise privately and then quickly move away so the student doesn't have to handle feelings of success by self-conscious behavior.

It may be useful to know a parent's hopes, fears and expectations for a student; what the parent can and cannot do with and for a child; the standards of learning achievement and behavior in the home, how these are taught, enforced and remediated; and how parents let their child know they're pleased or displeased with performance.

Critical to an educational plan is information as to whether the child is seen as "really great," "all right," or as an essentially "failing" person in the family.

2. For Assessing School Program Effectiveness

To assess the effectiveness of our educational work, it is useful to learn from parents the child's responses to what happened at school:

"Rudy can't wait to come to school since the science project started."

"Bill doesn't sleep well and complains of feeling ill since he was changed to a different group."

"Janet told her mother about making new friends after the teacher assigned her to work on projects with certain students."

"Helen displayed with pride a certificate for improved behavior in the lunchroom."

EDUCATIONALLY USELESS INFORMATION

Information which does not lead to productive planning not only is useless, it wastes conference time. That grandpa didn't read may be interesting, but probably won't help the teacher work more effectively with his grandchild. If a student has not yet learned to make friends with other children, to know that mother also was "shy" only suggests that mother may be accepting or excusing this behavior. The teacher still needs to develop ways to help the child learn necessary social skills.

Parents often give explanations of why their child does what (s)he does in the same way that we find "reasons" for our own and others' behaviors. Interestingly, the same behaviors are "explained" as being caused by the student being the first born, the last born, the middle or the only child, a boy or a girl. Some explanations may be right, others are farfetched or folktales. The only time an "explanation" is useful is when it suggests what might be done to solve the problem.

INFORMATION GETTING TECHNIQUES

When seeking information, it must be conveyed to the parent that we are searching for greater understanding of a student or situation in order to work with the youngster in the best possible way. Most parents will give the information if:

1. *They are convinced that it will be used in a way which helps their child.* It is important that the teacher establish a thoroughly professional "set" which assures the parent that the teacher is not prying or trying to find excuses for not having done well with the student or "entrapping" anyone, but is looking for helpful information.

16

2. ***Parents understand why the teacher is seeking information.***   A brief, frank statement about the area of concern will suffice. "Paula is such a bright girl and seemed turned on at school. But since vacation it is as if nothing interests her and she couldn't care less. I'm at a loss to understand why."

3. ***Teachers avoid getting into "who's to blame."***   Sometimes parents react in a "I'm not to blame" way because they bring to the conference the "set" of "We're going to be blamed for our child's lack of. . . . ," or because a complaint about the student is implied by the teacher's voice or manner, or in the way the teacher formulated the request for information. At the first hint that the conference might become focused on "who's to blame or not to blame," it is best to say: "Let's not waste time looking for where to put the blame. That won't help us to figure out what's best for your child now. Let's spend our time understanding him/her and the situation as best we can so that we can plan for his/her successful growth."

4. ***Teachers use phrases which encourage parents to share what they know about their child***   such as:
    Help me to know. . . .
    I can't seem to understand. . . .
    Can you shed light on. . . .
    I'm puzzled. . . .
    I'm at a loss to know. . . .
    I can't figure out what to make of. . . .

ELICITING USEFUL INFORMATION
1. *Requests for Specific Information*
Sometimes we have a specific concern:
> "Johnny hasn't looked well lately. Is there anything which would be helpful for me to know so that I don't expect too much or too little from him?"

> "Paul rarely talks in class. I'm wondering whether you also find him very quiet at home or whether there is something in the school situation which makes it hard for him to feel comfortable enough to say what he wants?"

> "Could you help me to know any special interests Susan has? I would like to give her more opportunities to work on things that she cares or knows a lot about. I've asked her but she hasn't come up with anything."

> "I'm puzzled about one of Beth's reactions. When I tell her she's done a fine job or in any way compliment her, she turns her head away or acts as if she just doesn't know what to do with praise. Would you tell me how you let Beth know when you're pleased with her? I want to be sure she's comfortable with my ways and if they're very different from yours, it would help me to be aware of that."

2. *Requests for General Information*

At times we cannot formulate precise questions. We are puzzled. Something just isn't making sense. In this case we tell the parents that we want to brainstorm for a while to see whether some information will emerge that triggers an idea in either of us. The term "fishing expedition" describes the nonspecific search for potentially helpful information.

For example, one teacher was puzzled by a kindergartner who alternated between being withdrawn, morose, sad, and being quite active and "with it." In the conference, information from the mother alerted the teacher to the possibility of an intermittent hearing loss due to allergies. This possibility was investigated, found to exist, and treated with excellent results.

Fishing expeditions have given clues which resulted in teachers' programming rest periods for students, changing or instituting reinforcers for fulfilling responsibilities and devising more effective ways of informing parents of student improvement.

It is to be expected that not all fishing expeditions will result in a useful "catch" of information or hints as to how to proceed. When despite all efforts, both parent and teacher remain baffled, the parent deserves to be told that the teacher is equally at a loss. The quandary is mutual. "Let's both keep watching and thinking about it and hopefully one of us will come up with something that will work."

PSEUDO REQUESTS

Teachers need to be careful that they do not use the deceptive practice of *pseudo* or *non* questions which, in the guise of asking for information, inform parents of problems (sometimes with a hidden message of accusation). Examples:

"Rob has not turned in homework for weeks. He says he has no time to do it either in the afternoon or at night. I thought I'd ask you about it."

"I'm puzzled about Susie's reaction to reading. She seems bright, but she gets so upset in the reading group she isn't able to sit still, keep her eyes focused on the page or remember what we're doing. Could you or her father possibly be putting more pressure on her than she can cope with at present?"

In both of the above examples, the teacher had information for the parent. To disguise it as a question, at best confuses the issue and the parent; at worst the negative inference may cause the parent to feel "put down."

FEEDBACK TO PARENTS

The best feedback for parents is to know that their information developed into concrete plans to help their child. Consequently, when parents supply useful information, they need to be told so; the more specifically the better. "Telling me about Bill's paper route helped me to make math more meaningful to him." "Your description of Mary at home helps me to know why she often becomes discouraged."

Information getting conferences should conclude with a brief statement of appreciation for the information, how the information will be used, what, if anything, needs to be done further by home or school, and how and when parent and teacher, in their ongoing partnership, will inform the other of changes in student behaviors.

What shall we do about. . . . ?

THE PROBLEM SOLVING CONFERENCE

Many learning and behavior problems respond best to interventions jointly designed and acted upon by teachers and parents. The wish "If only I could get those parents to work with me" reflects many teachers' awareness of the desirability of parental collaboration to increase student learning.

Teachers also are often painfully aware of the fact that some parents lack the knowledge and skills in child rearing or managing home routines. As a result, their children may not have learned what other children are taught at home. Sometimes, teachers can help parents acquire some of those skills. This may appear to be a formidable task (it certainly is not an easy one), but it is possible to accomplish because techniques of teaching apply to adults as well as to children and many parents want to become more skilled in helping their child succeed.

It is essential to emphasize that, *regardless of the home and what is done or not done there, the school cannot relinquish responsibility for doing a quality educational job* with each child. Consequently, the school cannot "buck pass" or take the position, "You straighten your kids out and then we can teach them." Schools must accept responsibility for developing the best possible educational program for each student regardless of his/her home life. As an *adjunct to that educational program*, the problem solving conference can help parents to do something that will increase the probability of the student becoming more productive.

Situations which benefit from home-school collaboration fall into three categories:

1. *The student is not physically and/or emotionally available for learning.*
   Examples:

   Betty is frequently late for school. The parents need to *do* something so that she is on time and ready for learning when school begins.

   Maxine can't see the blackboard clearly (or the words on the written page) without glasses. The parents need to make sure she has glasses and brings them to school.

   Harold seems so fatigued he has little energy to learn. Parents need to insure more adequate rest.

   Milton needs to be cleaner or have clothes that fit comfortably. His parents need to take care of this.

   Anne is rarely pleased with any of her work. It would help if her parents express greater satisfaction with what she has accomplished rather than express concern about what she has not yet learned.

2. *The student needs additional practice or additional exposures to certain experiences.*

Examples:

Susie needs reading practice. It would be helpful if she read to her parents daily from books suggested by her teacher.

Ginny is deficient in eye-hand coordination. She would benefit from playing ball and from cutting, pasting and tracing at home.

Howard does not grasp math easily. It would help him to learn that math has real life implications through measuring cookie ingredients or setting the table "for so many people" or budgeting and spending an allowance.

Murray acts as if he is not aware that he can do things for himself. If the parents gave him more home responsibilities and rewarded his increasing skills in meeting them, that feeling of competence might transfer into more independence in the classroom.

Kate needs to feel that what she says is important. It could help if the family showed they valued her expressions by listening more carefully, and by responding to and respecting her thoughts, observations or feelings.

3. *The student needs acknowledgement of and recognition of improvement in behavior.*

Parents are powerful "significant others" for their children. At times, parents' approval and disapproval are more influential than any recognition the school can give, and, given appropriately, will greatly enhance their child's achievement both in and out of school. Teachers and parents need to insure that students get desirable reinforcement for productive behaviors and strong reasons for discontinuing unproductive ones. This necessitates that parents are informed about how their youngster is doing through periodic phone calls, notes* or checklists.

Examples:

Billy may get his work done if he has to take a brief note home each day about how "good a worker he was." Teacher and parents agreed that four good notes per week mean that he can stay up later on Friday night to watch a favorite TV program.

To encourage Doug to solve problems without hitting, he keeps a diary of his feelings and records the number of "peaceful" recesses and noon periods. He shows the record to his father who encourages him and takes him along on weekend errands, which Doug enjoys. (Additionally, Doug gets writing practice and practice in dealing with angry feelings by expressing them in words.)

Joan has developed superb skills in disrupting the class and precious few skills in following the teacher's directions. It would help her to improve if the parents worked with the school in carrying through with definite, positive consequences for self-control and negative consequences for lack of it.

---

*An example of a teacher's weekly note to a parent on page 102.

Most problems are not solved by merely reporting them to parents. "He's always tardy," "He disrupts the class by his antics," "He can't sit still," are only statements which describe a situation of which the parent usually is painfully aware. The parent may know, for instance, when tardy Johnny ought to be ready to leave for school, but may not know, and therefore needs to learn, *what to do* to get that accomplished.

A teacher's admonitions or "you shoulds" won't solve the problem either. Telling a smothering mother to let her son more often experience his own successes and failures will be futile if she does not know, and therefore needs to learn, what to do instead of what she is doing. Or a father, whose only response to misbehavior is to punish his son, will not be able to stop that punishment until he has learned more successful ways to get his boy to mind.

For Johnny who is tardy and whose mother indicates it's because he dawdles getting dressed, it may become the teacher's job to *teach* mother how to *teach* Johnny to get ready on time. Just as in teaching a new skill to a student, the teacher needs to explain, model, discuss, and possibly role play in order to teach each step of the process to the parent. An example will be given later in this chapter.

In teaching a parent a new skill, we need to:

a) Prepare parents for the probability of initial frustrations. There is a long step between working something out in a conference and putting it into operation in the home, just as there is a long step between initial teaching and a student's successful performance. Subsequent to the conference, the parent may encounter pressures which push back recall of what was discussed, or (s)he simply may not understand each step as fully as (s)he had thought (just like students in school). Parents may chafe at the time it takes their child to learn to do something well and at their own lack of teaching skills. They may be like the young student teacher, eager to try but woefully inexperienced as yet in how to "bring it off."

b) Plan to support parents. Parents need reassurances that the school will continue to work with and support them and, as they persist, most likely they will learn "to do it" with increasing proficiency and success.

c) Select, *one and only one* area on which to focus parents' effort at any one time. If Johnny is chronically tardy, has not yet learned how to make friends, has poor motor coordination, and a number of other problem behaviors, the temptation will be to clean up the whole mess in one fell swoop. We need to resist the idea of trying to tackle everything. If the decision is first to work on getting a child in class when the bell rings, we need to concentrate on what each of us will do to achieve the goal. Other problems can wait to be taken up at a future time when the first problem is more nearly solved. The skills we learn from working together will speed up solutions of subsequent problems.

Teachers who feel inadequate to help parents increase their child rearing skills can learn what parents can do through books,* or consultations with more experienced teachers, parents or other professionals.

Following is an outline of the steps necessary for a parent to become a collaborator in helping a child to learn or behave better:

1. Identification of the student's *school* behavior which needs changing.
2. Determination of what the teacher will do at school.

---

*See *Improving Your Child's Behavior*. Madeline Hunter and Paul V. Carlson. TIP Publications, P.O. Box 514, El Segundo, California 90245. 1977.

3. Identification of student behaviors at home which are the same or contribute to the problem.

4. Identification of parent behaviors which may accentuate the problem.

5. Agreement by the parent to *do* something which is both productive and within his/her ability.

6. Identification of alternative actions by the parents and selection of those which are both feasible and promising in altering the student's behaviors.

7. Selection of the reinforcers* which are likely to promote improvements in the student's behavior.

8. Instruction, step by step, in how to put the plan into effect.

9. *Action* by the parents in the home.

10. Follow-up by teacher for feedback, support, evaluation, help with snags.

The steps in this outline work equally well when the parent initiates the request for teacher help to ameliorate a home problem such as "I can't get him to bed early enough so I can get him up in the morning."

Following is a summary of these steps in a conference which contributed to the solution of the problem of a boy who was chronically late for school.

1) The teacher described the behavior as it affected the learning situation. "Sandy usually is late for school. As a result, he doesn't know what's going on so he is out of step with the rest of the class and becomes mischievous."

2) To increase his desire to be on time the teacher planned to schedule one of Sandy's favorite subjects first in the morning, and to reinforce his being on time.

3) The teacher probed for additional helpful information about what happened at home in the morning. She learned that mother gets Sandy up in plenty of time to be ready for school, but he dawdles getting dressed.

4) The teacher learned that Mother admonishes, nags and threatens, but "nothing happens."

5) The teacher got a commitment from Mother to *do* something which promised to be more useful than her previous actions.

6) Teacher and mother generated a series of feasible alternatives which might change Sandy's dawdling behavior. From those they selected the ones that seemed most likely to work. Those were:

> Mother or Sandy will select his clothes the evening before. He will have the kitchen timer in his room to remind him of how many minutes are left until he must be ready to leave the house.
>
> Mother will prohibit morning TV until he is dressed, has had breakfast, and has all his things ready for school.

7) Teacher and mother discussed which motivators and reinforcers would increase the likelihood that Sandy would be speedier. Those were:

> He will have a chart on which he marks each day he's ready to leave for school on time.

---

*See *Reinforcement Theory for Teachers*. Madeline Hunter. TIP Publications, P.O. Box 514, El Segundo, California 90245. 1967.

For every 5 marks he will earn a special privilege to be selected by him and his family (such as choosing what the family will have for dinner or taking a friend to a show).

No check mark on a day will delay his special privileges.

Mother *will not check on him nor nag, frown or fume*, even if he's slow. The teacher will handle his lateness when he arrives.

Mother will praise him, in ways he likes, for his cooperation, speediness, grown-up behaviors: "I'm amazed, I surely didn't think you could do it that fast. Wait till I tell Dad about how you've learned to get dressed in just a few minutes."

8) In the conference, mother and teacher went over the plan of action step by step. Nothing was taken for granted. The teacher asked questions such as: "How will you let Sandy know what he is to do?" "When might be a good time to get started?" "How will he know what to expect from you?" "What will you say to him?" constantly explaining, role playing, modeling or giving examples.

The plan included the actual words which could be used to explain the new morning procedure to Sandy at a time when both he and mother were unhurried and calm. "I've talked with your teacher. We've planned some new things to help you be on time for school." Sunday morning was the time chosen for mother to talk with Sandy and to provide a practice session which included going through all the getting-ready-for-school steps. The kitchen timer was used to see how long it took him to get dressed without dawdling. It was a real dry run in which he was setting his own time.

Mother would praise Sandy for his cooperation. She would *not* make any negative remarks such as, "I've always known you could do it if you wanted to."

9) At the end of the conference, having a definite plan, mother needed to go home and *act*.

When parents experience immediate success in working more productively with their youngsters, they are highly reinforced to continue their efforts. However, as stated earlier, often there are initial difficulties. Therefore, the teaching role with parents needs to be similar to the one we assume when students are learning something new at school. After instruction, we check on their understanding, reteach and give assistance if needed, and reinforce performance.

10) As a follow-up, after the plan had been put into effect, mother phoned the teacher to report how things were going. This enabled the teacher to iron out snags, replan, and support the parent by acknowledging the effort it takes to effect changes.

At the same time, the teacher reported to the parent that there were positive changes in Sandy's behavior at school. By being on time in the morning, he was more successfully participating in activities throughout the day.

During the second week after the plan had been in effect, the teacher reported again by telephone. After that, an occasional note saying how well Sandy was doing, now that he was at school on time, helped to prevent back-sliding. The teacher's follow-up with support, encouragement, and skilled help increased the probability of success.

Systematic and professional "joining hands with parents" will go a long way towards solving many problems requiring home-school collaboration. Occasionally, however, the problem is such that professional help beyond the school's capacity is indicated. In these cases, the problem should be referred to the principal, nurse, counselor or other professional school person who is qualified to make the appropriate prescriptive referral (see page 82).

Section II   CONFERENCING SKILLS

5. REASONABLE EXPECTATIONS
   What can be accomplished in one conference?   25

6. ESTABLISHING THE CONFERENCE OBJECTIVE
   Are we agreed on our focus?   27

7. PREPARATION FOR CONFERENCES
   What do I do to get ready?   31

8. OPENING STATEMENTS
   How do I start?   33

9. FORMULATING THE MESSAGE
   How do I say it?   34

10. THE CHECK-BACK
    What did you hear?   42

11. CLOSING THE CONFERENCE
    How do I end?   44

12. JUDGING THE SUCCESS OF A CONFERENCE
    How did it go?   46

REASONABLE EXPECTATIONS

Both parents and teachers can be unrealistic in their expectations as to what can be accomplished in a single conference. "They don't understand and I explained it completely," or "I've told them what needed to be done and they're still not doing it," are understandable expressions of frustration, but may not be reasonable expectations of conference results.

Limitations exist as to what can be accomplished by one conference. Expectations need to match 1) the amount of time available, 2) the teacher's skills, 3) the receptivity of the parent at the time of the conference, and 4) the complexity of the message.

1. *The Amount of Time Available*

If the time we have available for a parent is short and conferences are infrequent, the objectives that can be achieved are limited (just as we would need to plan a simple rather than elaborate meal if we had only a short time to prepare it).

Granted, the more skilled the teacher, the more effectively time will be used. It takes time, however, to get to know another person and to find words which will be meaningful. It takes time for something to be said, heard, explored, digested. It takes time to develop trust and understanding so that teacher and parent together can look sensitively at a child and determine what, under the circumstances, might be best. *It takes an even longer time to put a plan into effect and for changes to occur.*

Some school systems seem neither to recognize the need for, nor value the expenditure of, the time it takes to work effectively with parents. Nor do many school systems realize that conferencing, because it requires a high level of professional performance, is a drain on teacher energy and, as a result, requires an augmentation or diversion of energy from teachers' more obvious daily responsibilities with students.

It is necessary for school districts, teachers and parents to acknowledge that an adequate amount of time, when teacher and parent are free of other demands, is essential for successful home-school collaboration.

2. *The Skills of the Teacher*

Conferencing skills are such a critical determiner of both what and how much can be accomplished that this book was written to enhance those communicative skills and thereby increase the potential for achievement of conference objectives.

3. *The Parent's Emotional Receptivity*

Is the parent relaxed, comfortable with him/herself, not easily upset by the behaviors and needs of growing children? Is the parent flexible and open so that (s)he takes in new information and modifies concepts and ideas? Or is the parent closed, defensive, not trusting of self or others, threatened by children's behaviors, or feeling inadequate or awed in the presence of teachers?

Is the parent "with it" at the time of the conference or is (s)he tired, consumed with other concerns, or "blinded" by apprehensions related to the conference? What might have seemed reasonable expectations in planning, may become over- or underestimates of what can be accomplished and may have to be adjusted during the conference.

4. *The Complexity of the Message or Task for That Parent*

Sometimes the message to be delivered is a very complex one (for example, the student of normal or above ability who for some unknown reason does not learn), or the task for which the parent is asked to become responsible is an exceedingly delicate and difficult one, (for example, conveying increased expectations for the student's performance without implying dissatisfaction with previous efforts and accomplishments).

Parents' wide range of abilities to respond to these messages and tasks indicate there are differences in what we might reasonably expect will result from a conference. Some tasks, easily learned by one parent are "horrendously difficult" for another; some messages are welcomed or taken in stride by one family and are almost impossible for the next one to handle.

If we sensibly match our expectations for what we would like to accomplish to the time available, the emotional state of the parents, the complexity of the message or task, and the parents' abilities, unrealistic expectations with their inevitable disappointments will more frequently be avoided.

Additionally, as professionals and as citizens, we need to insure that our administrators and school boards increasingly take cognizance of the fact that, in order to promote our students' learning, we spend considerable professional time with some of their parents. We need time to conference, help to promote our own conferencing skills and recognition of the vital importance of that aspect of our work.

Are we agreed on our focus?

ESTABLISHING THE CONFERENCE OBJECTIVE

When conference participants are focused on different concerns or have different ideas about what they want to accomplish and do not make those differences explicit, the time spent can be wasteful or disappointing.

Teacher and parent come together as consenting adults. Each has to clearly convey to the other, "I'm here to talk about _____." Then both have to agree that that is a productive use of time. Otherwise, both may leave frustrated, "Nothing was accomplished. (S)he did not understand, did not care about what is important, is not willing to '*do* something'."

Regardless of whether the conference is initiated at home or at school, to avoid disappointments, teacher and parent need to go through the process of establishing objectives for the conference by:

1. Knowing their own wishes for the use of conference time.
2. Stating these clearly.
3. Acknowledging possible differences.
4. Reaching an agreement as to how the time together will be spent.

The objectives a parent and a teacher have for any conference, can be either mutually agreeable or they can differ.

Mutually agreeable objectives. Most conferences have mutually agreeable objectives. For example, the teacher plans to give a student progress report to the parent. The parent knows this, and comes to school with that objective in mind.

Or, the teacher believes that a particular student, in order to become more motivated to improve computational skills, needs to learn ways that arithmetic has a practical everyday use. The parent is agreeable to this focus for the conference. The teacher then explains to the parent the kind of help needed: handling money, budgeting, shopping for the family groceries, etc.

Parents also initiate conferences that have objectives agreeable to teachers. One parent may ask for suggestions of appropriate reading materials, another for specific information on some aspect of a child's performance or development. Many ask how they can help their child with homework.

Even in routine reporting conferences, however, interests may vary as to the emphasis placed on certain aspects of the student's performance. A parent may be concerned with the speed of computational skills while the teacher may be focusing on the application of those skills to word problems. A mother may be more eager to know the student's social development (is (s)he now making friends and are those friendships productive?) while the teacher is concerned by lack of growth in an academic area. Or it can be math, reading, physical development or behavior in general that concerns the parent rather than the student's ability to function in a group.

Prior to a reporting conference, it is helpful to ask parents about their preference as to emphasis (see page 97). Then those preferences can be used to initiate communication. "You said you were concerned about Paul's clumsiness on the playground. I've watched him carefully and I've had our coach also take a look. Here's what we plan to do and you might help by _____."

Without prior indications of parental preference, we begin the conference by asking the parents whether they have a special interest: "The purpose of our conference today is to give you an overall picture of how Robert is doing in school, what he is particularly strong in, what he needs to work on, and how he generally gets along. Will you tell me whether you're especially interested in certain areas so that I am sure to cover those well?" If the parent indicates a preference, we would begin there; if not, we would proceed according to our own plan.

Differing objectives. Sometimes the perception of what is most important to talk about differs between parent and teacher. For example, a teacher may be concerned about the inability of a student to pay attention. The parent, however, is concerned about the child's reading group because it is not "challenging."

A teacher may be concerned about the student's use of inappropriate language. The parents are determined not to "squelch his/her emotional freedom to express him/herself."

Sometimes, teachers are concerned about the "state of the learner" and parents about "the state of the school." Resolution of those different objectives need to be achieved as it is unlikely both can be satisfactorily dealt with in one conference.

Let's examine two ways of dealing with the dilemma of differing objectives:

1. *Resolution through allotment of conference time for each concern or scheduling a subsequent conference to meet one of the objectives.*

"We'll divide today's time so we handle both your concern and mine and see how that works out. If we run out of time, we'll make another appointment to pick up what we were not able to get done today."

For example, in a reporting conference, a teacher's objective is to give information about the child. Sometimes, the parent asks about the solution to a problem, "What can I do about _____?" or "How do you handle _____?"

With time inadequate to accomplish both objectives, the teacher has to choose one of three alternatives:

   a. Accept the parents objective. "If you want to talk about _____ today, I'll be happy to do that. We'll make another appointment to tell you about _____'s progress."
   b. Describe the student's progress and make a subsequent appointment to discuss the parent's concern. "If it's all right with you, today let's talk about how _____ is doing in school. But let's set a time as soon as possible to discuss your concern."
   c. Identify the two possibilities and let the parent make the choice. "We can discuss your concern about _____ now and make another appointment for a progress report, or I can report to you today, and we can get together again soon to talk about your questions. Which would you prefer?"

No one solution is always best. Each has merits; the teacher must assess the situation to determine which one seems most promising.

2. *Resolution of differing objectives through developing a new conference objective which will resolve the divergence and is agreeable to both parent and teacher.*

When two objectives are not discrete, but present different views, interpretations or solutions to the same concern, this resolution is useful. An alternative conference objective is best found by exploring the facts. Is there a common concern? What options for action do school and home have? What consequences might result from each of those options? The most logical, productive solution or the one with the least undesirable consequences then has a chance to become apparent. Seeking that solution becomes the objective of the conference.

Let's look at an example of such a resolution of divergent objectives:

Mrs. Green, Mary's mother, comes in to complain that the girl is not in a high enough reading group and is bored. The teacher had concluded that Mary needed to work on comprehension skills and, therefore, had placed her in a group where the difficulty of the vocabulary would not present a problem.

Mrs. Green's objective for the conference is to have Mary's reading group changed. The teacher's objective is to have Mrs. Green understand and support the educational plan for Mary. Because of the difference in objectives, the teacher may be tempted to do one of three things, none of which will be in Mary's best interest: 1) accede to the mother's request, 2) pass the buck by asking the principal or the reading specialist to make the decision, 3) tell Mrs. Green that the assigned group is best for Mary.

If the teacher either gives in or buck passes, (s)he is abdicating responsibility as the professional best qualified to make educational decisions. Mary's mother also is denied the opportunity to gain understanding of how the teacher plans to promote reading growth. The problem with the teacher being adamant about what is best for Mary is that Mrs. Green probably will not be listening to the teacher, but waiting for a chance to tell what she thinks.

The best course would be the identification of a new conference objective, one which would involve exploring available options, anticipating the consequences that could result from each, and then selecting the one that appears to be the most productive for Mary's growth and mother's satisfaction.

The teacher might say to Mrs. Green, "It will help if you tell me why you don't think the group is good for her. And I will tell you why I placed her there. Then, let's explore what the consequences might be for Mary if she were in the higher reading group as you suggest and the consequences if we leave her in the group into which I placed her. By doing that, we can look at what she might gain or lose in either placement and decide what might be best for her."

Many parents would agree to give this a try. There is no guarantee that either participant will convince the other. However, the discussion gives the parent a chance to gain an understanding of what the teacher believes the student needs to learn, as well as knowledge of the care and concern with which the teacher makes educational decisions. The teacher, on the other hand, may learn how the parent perceives the child, what values or pressure exist in the home, and the parent's fears, even if unfounded. Neither teacher or parent has anything to lose through this approach and much to gain.

Changing Objectives During a Conference. Just as educational objectives are changed during the course of a classroom lesson when the planned objective is inappropriate or when a more valuable objective emerges, the original conference objective can be modified or discarded for a better one. Indeed, such revisions often are essential to successful communication. New information or new insights can make the original objective no longer pertinent or valid. Sometimes objectives turn out to be overambitious and impossible to accomplish, or the intended objective may appear less urgent than does an emerging one.

Should a change of objective be made during the conference, it is essential that the change be verbally acknowledged so that both parties in the interchange are aware of and agreeable to that change.

The following is an example of an information getting conference in which the original objective was accomplished almost immediately and a new objective agreed upon.

The teacher needed information about a listless, withdrawn kindergarten child. She opened the conference with, "I'm very puzzled about Sylvia. At school, she sits quietly most of the time chewing on a pencil or looking around. She doesn't get into the other children's activities and games. I need to know how you see her at home—whatever you can tell me about her that might help me to understand how better to plan for her." As soon as the teacher stated her objective, the father asked, "Is it true that premature children often do not catch up for a number of years?" The teacher had not been aware that the girl was premature. The birth weight on the girl's health card had been misread for 7.7 lbs. instead of 2.7 lbs. This new information shifted the objective of the conference from information getting (the essential information had been identified) to making suitable plans for the girl.

Consequently, the teacher redefined the objective: "You have given me very important information. It may be that Sylvia hasn't yet caught up with other children her age. You may want to discuss this again with your own or the school doctor. In the meantime, why don't we make the assumption that she should not be expected to meet every requirement of other children her age. Let's talk about a program that might be best for her and how we both could provide that." The parent was agreeable. As a result, the girl, with agreement from the school doctor and counselor, was given the opportunity to participate for a part of each day in a special program where she could begin to close the developmental gap.

In summary, it is important that the objective of every conference be identified and agreed upon. An advance query or a question at the beginning of the conference can determine parents' interests or concerns. The teacher should incorporate this information in the formulation and articulation of the conference objectives. In case of differing or mutually exclusive objectives, apportioning time for each objective, scheduling an additional conference or developing a third, mutually agreeable objective, usually resolves the differences and results in more satisfying and productive communication.

PREPARATION FOR CONFERENCES

Preparation for conferencing is as important as preparation for teaching. Lack of success in either often can be attributed to insufficient or faulty planning.

Preparation for an Introductory Group Conference

In anticipation of a get acquainted group conference, the teacher needs to:

1. Invite the parents to the meeting. Invitation should be sent with sufficient lead time so parents can make arrangements to attend and so the teacher can consider the questions parents would like answered. (See *sample invitation*, page 96)

2. Determine what to include or exclude from the meeting so as to stay within the time allotted, and formulate ways to give that information clearly. This is difficult because usually there is more to say than parents can absorb in any one meeting.

3. Select appropriate descriptions and examples of student work that tell, in ways parents can understand, about the program and what students will learn.

4. From the questions sent in by parents, include those which are meaningful to the group.

5. Think of tactful responses for those parents who insist on discussing their child or personal concern so as to graciously but clearly convey the message, "not now."

6. Plan how to end the conference on time, no matter how many eager parents ask to have "just one more" question considered.

Preparation for a Reporting Conference

In anticipation of a reporting conference, the teacher needs to:

1. Secure auxiliary data.

It is advisable to read records and consult with others at school who are acquainted with the student or the family. Conference hopes or fears that are unrealistically high or low can be adjusted by knowledge of how the student has functioned in the past, how (s)he is currently functioning in different school settings, and how the family typically functions. Caution is needed not to use this information prejudicially, but as an aid to understanding and working productively in the present situation.

2. Determine information to be given the parent which should include:
   a. Significant aspects of the student which are to be described.
   b. Routine aspects which are to be reported.
   c. Examples of school work or behavior which will best document or clarify verbal descriptions and the number of examples that are "just enough."

3. Organize the information.

Many teachers find it helpful to make a brief conference outline with a few main reference points they wish to cover and include ideas of the most understandable and enabling ways to describe the student's achievements. This outline then becomes a guide or "road map" for use during the conference.

4. Determine the student's participation in the conference.

Even though the student's participation in the conference cannot be determined solely by the teacher (the student's and parent's wishes need to be taken into account), the teacher needs to make the final decisions about:

a. The amount of time the student will be present in the conference.

b. The responsibility the student will assume (listening only, giving one or more reports, interacting throughout the conference).

c. The preparation of the student for participation.

d. If the student is not present in the conference, the person(s) who will tell the student what was discussed.

e. The most enabling way that information can be given to the student.

Preparation for an Information-Getting Conference

In anticipation of an information-getting conference, the teacher needs to:

1. Determine how to state the concern about the student.

2. Identify corroborative or descriptive data (student work, observations by others in the school, anectodal records) which will make the concern more understandable to the parent.

3. Formulate questions that have potential for eliciting the information needed.

4. Decide whether knowing before the conference what information is being sought would help the parent to organize thoughts and observations or create undue anxiety.

5. Devise ways to assure the parent that information will be used in the best interest of the student.

6. Determine responses that will tell the parent when information is useful.

Preparation for a Problem Solving Conference

In anticipation of a problem solving conference, the teacher needs to:

1. Determine ways to describe the problem that have high probability of eliciting collaboration.

2. Describe what the school has done to lessen the problem, what the results have been, and what the school is not able to do that appears to be needed.

3. Identify what the parent could do that might help and determine ways to communicate that information.

4. Plan ways to find out if the parent needs to learn new insights or skills in order to help.

5. Determine how to give assistance to the parent if it is needed.

6. If support is needed by the parent after the conference, anticipate how this can be accomplished.

7. Determine what student behaviors will constitute evidence of success.

Careful preparation for conferences is time consuming but, in the end is time saving in accomplishing the purpose of any conference. Adequate preparation enables the teacher to work efficiently. An effective report meaningfully describes the class program or the student's accomplishments with examples devoid of tangential or imprecise information, and identifies areas for collaboration or concern. Preparation also will help parents give useful information because what they are asked to think about and convey will be clear to them. As a result, careful preparation enables teachers and parents to work as a problem solving team for the benefit of students.

OPENING STATEMENTS

The tone setting power of an opening statement cannot be overemphasized. It conveys the teacher's attitude toward both the parent and the importance of the conference as well as sets the stage for subsequent interaction.

Some teachers feel comfortable starting with small talk. "Did you have a good summer?" "We thoroughly enjoyed the cookies." Small talk, however, is best kept to a minimum because the work of the conference begins only when we start professional communication.

For conferences initiated by either parent or teacher, it is helpful to develop and practice a few variations of opening statements so that they feel comfortable, are easily available, and provide an overture to the statement of purpose for the conference.

Examples for teacher initiated conferences:

"I'm glad you had time to come in today. I wanted to talk to you about _____."

"Thank you for coming. I've been puzzled about _____ and I need your help."

"I'm glad to see you. I thought you would want to know that _____."

"I've been looking forward to talking with you. As you know, the main reason for our conference is _____."

Examples for parent initiated conferences:

"I'm glad you called to set up this meeting"—then wait for the parent to take over.

"I'm glad to see you. What would you like to discuss?"

Whenever parents request conference time, full attention should first be given to their concerns. Even if we also have concerns, it is best to avoid a statement such as, "I'm glad to see you. I've wanted to call you myself about _____," because that takes the initiative away from the parent. However, if we find that both we and the parent have observed similar behaviors on the part of the student, sharing that information joins us in the same area of concern.

When our concern is different from that of the parent, the parent's need to talk should be satisfied before introducing an additional topic. Often it is better to arrange a subsequent meeting and not dilute the present interaction with our concern.

The first few moments in any interchange are particularly important. Consequently opening statements deserve thoughtful attention.

FORMULATING THE MESSAGE

Even though in our daily life we often settle for not being fully understood, we cannot afford the problems that result from misunderstandings in our professional encounters. While we can never completely insure full understanding, we will greatly increase that probability if we formulate our message in such a way that four conditions are met:

1. Our message must be in words that are familiar to parents so that they can make a *literal translation* into the meaning we intended. This is a parallel to the words, signals and examples we use in teaching which we match to the ability of the student to derive meanings from them.

2. Our message must describe the circumstances and conditions surrounding student behaviors so that parents can interpret them *in context.*

3. Our message includes *enabling phrases* that help the parent remain a participant in the communication.

4. The message does not contain emotionally laden words or phrases, *red flags* that can block communication.

1. *Literal Translation*
a) *Technical terms or jargon.*

The typical parent could not understand a report about their child's math accomplishments given to them in Sanscrit, no matter how cogently stated. Most parents are equally bewildered by, "Your child's reading skills are deficient in terms of the higher levels of Bloom's taxonomy. Consequently, our objective is that (s)he work on analysis, synthesis and evaluation."

When speaking with those outside of their profession, master communicators speak in everyday language. Use of jargon distances us from nonprofessionals with whom we speak.

Technical terms or jargon constitute a valid shorthand language developed by professionals for their *own* use. While most teachers would not report to parents in language as technical as our example, much of what is said to parents is phrased in language unfamiliar to them. Among educators, common terms which the typical parent cannot easily translate into meaning are: regrouping, decoding (in reading), behavioral or instructional objectives, cognitive, affective and psychomotor skills, focus, attending behaviors, limit setting, meeting (or not meeting) expectations, attention span, manipulative behavior, listening skills, adjustment, adaptive (or maladaptive) behaviors, self-concept, maturation level, ego strength, etc.

When technical terms are used, an explanation or translation into more common terms, understandable to parents, is essential. "Paul is beginning to use context clues, which means he is reading the other words and sentences around a new word and figuring out what it might be." "Sue is adding three place numbers with regrouping, or carrying as we used to call it, such as 149 plus 382." This could avoid the confusion reported when a parent who was told that her child had difficulty with regrouping asked, "Oh, did you change math groups *again?*"

34

b) *"Euphe-nothings"* (euphemisms, trite or "white-wash" statements, cliches). Some statements *seem* to describe an event but really don't because meaning cannot accurately be assigned by the listener. From actual records some of the writers' favorite "euphe-nothings" are:

The parents of a boy who was the playground terror unless everyone did what he wanted were told: "He has his own ideas about how games should be played and what the rules are."

The school bully was described as: "His contacts with other children are physical."

A child who had a hard time paying attention was reported to need to "improve her distractibility with peers."

Parents of a child whose stories were about people killing each other and dying painfully were told that "she often chooses to write stories with topics quite different from what other students would choose."

A disruptive student was described as "very active," a "busybody," "a little too social," and a painfully withdrawn student as "not talking very much in class."

One student gave everyone "fits" by finding excuse after excuse to avoid doing work and placing responsibility on someone else for whatever happened. The teacher reported to the parents: "Mary manipulates the environment for her own benefit." "Yes," responded the father, "That's what all successful people do and that's what makes for civilization."

Another teacher told a parent that his son "did not respect authority." The parent replied: "I know. I want him to have a strong, independent ego." The fact that the boy cursed the teacher, was openly defiant and didn't do his work was not described clearly so the parent interpreted the message as communicating a desirable trait.

If we were to listen to what we tell parents about their youngsters as if we, ourselves, heard it for the first time, would we hear an unambiguous description of the student? If we were the parents, could we create an accurate mind picture of the situation as the teacher sees it?

Even though we may have reported a continuing concern, some parents tell us: "I've never heard that before." At times, that may literally be true. They may not have been able to comprehend the meaning of what has been said to them because jargon or "euphe-nothings" have been used. At other times, they simply were not able to tolerate "receiving" the message.

2. *Contextual Translation*

The context in which behavior occurs assigns significance to it. A loud yell is appropriate when the favorite team wins. That same behavior is inappropriate at a church service or during a silent reading period. Therefore, if there is any chance of ambiguity, we need to explain the context in which we use words. "Fast" can mean speedy, very social, without food or water, or to tie something up. "Objective" can mean an unbiased observation or a goal. "Neat" can mean orderly or approved of. There are 25 dictionary definitions of the word "set."

If we say to a parent: "Sam hits" (a simple statement describing behavior), the parent has no way of knowing the significance we assign to that action. Does Sam hit because he is constantly at odds with others, or is it the typical behavior of a young child who has not yet learned that there are other responses he can use to get the attention of his peers, or does he think that's a way of showing he's "big." To overcome the ambiguity, we explain the context in which the behavior occurs.

"Sam came to school in September not yet interested in other children. Then he began to watch them and play alongside of them. Now he has begun to want to be with them. He hasn't as yet learned how to be noticed and invited to play, so, like many children who want to have other kids pay attention to them, he hits. We are teaching him to 'get in' with other children by saying, 'Let's play _____.' "

"Mary often works alone" could have different meanings in different contexts such as, 1) at choice time she prefers reading or painting to working on projects with others, 2) she is an independent learner, not needing much teacher supervision, 3) she has not yet learned to work cooperatively, 4) others don't choose her as a work mate.

Therefore, the intended meaning must be explained: "Mary often works alone. At choice time, her favorite activity is reading. However, she always is very productive in activities where she needs to work with others such as committee work and planning our mural and she has many friends. Mary is one of those people who is comfortable alone, yet enjoys others."

At times, misperceptions, arising from the way words are used, can be funny. A teacher conferenced with a mother about the child's morning tardiness. The teacher wondered whether it was hard for the mother to get the family ready and out of the house in the morning and asked, "Is this an area which is difficult for you?" "No," replied the mother, "not here, but when I lived in another neighborhood it was hard. I had such a long way to walk to school and to the store."

To avoid any possible ambiguity as to the significance of behavior we describe or terms we use, we need to add sufficient contextual explanation so that parents know our meanings.

3. Enabling Phrases

To enable parents to stay in collaborative communication with us and to avoid creating emotional distance, we include in our messages: a) invitational statements, b) time-referenced statements, c) positive comments to parents about their contributions to the conference, d) supportive comments to parents who experience difficulties in raising their youngsters, e) comments that keep the conference on focus.

a. *Invitational statements.*

An invitational statement invites the parent into a partnership to investigate an issue which needs special attention. Although often used in reporting conferences, invitational statements are a particularly important part of information getting and problem solving conferences.

Examples:

"I'm puzzled"

"I'm at a loss to know _____."

"Help me to understand _____."

"I don't seem to be able to put something together about _____."

"I've thought a lot about _____ lately, and I'm still not sure about some things."

"Maybe you can help me to see things more clearly."

"Could you shed some light on _____."

"I can't figure out what to make of _____."

"So far I haven't been able to think of _____."

b. *Time-referenced statements.*

Much of what all of us do changes in time. The time-referenced statement indicates that possibility and softens the implication of a static "(s)he is," sounding as if "(s)he will always be that way."

Saying "Johnny *still* needs to learn to get close to other children," or "Johnny seems not to have know-how *as yet* to _____" is time-referenced. "Johnny doesn't have friends," or "He has no friends," sounds as if it's final. "At this time," or "right now," or "(s)he still feels scared to try something new" is time-referenced. "He's an anxious child" sounds permanent, and is name-calling (see page 39).

Time-referenced statements, by indicating a child is a growing and emerging human being, enable parents to stay in contact emotionally with us. Behavior exhibited *now* may well be transitory. Their child can and probably will learn new behaviors if assisted by supportive team work of parents and teachers.

Examples:

"Sam hasn't yet learned (or doesn't yet have the know-how)."

"At this time _____."

"S/he still needs to come to terms with (or still feels, or needs to _____)."

"Right now _____."

"While (s)he's learning (s)he _____."

When using time-referenced statements, it is important that we do not white-wash or inadvertently give the impression that the described behavior is of little significance and will, with no work on our part, change, unless that is exactly what we mean to convey. Teachers and parents have waited for years for certain students' undesirable phases to pass. They didn't because no one made it clear that different behaviors were expected and no one taught those behaviors.

c. *Positive Comments to Parents about their Contributions to the Conference*

Many parents come to conferences with feelings ranging from uneasiness to fear. These feelings can block communication. Conventional phrases such as "Thank you for coming," or "I'm glad to see you" may be insufficient to "free" such parents. Therefore, specific feedback throughout the conference to let parents know their presence and contribution are valued can give the needed continuing support.

The following statements can be used to acknowledge the importance of the parents' contributions and give positive feedback:

> "You're really perceptive to have noticed _____."
>
> "I'm glad to know about that."
>
> "I'm glad you thought to tell me _____."
>
> "You surely know your child well."
>
> "How wise of you to look at it that way."
>
> "This sounds important. I'm glad you brought it up."

These comments also help to "shape" the conference. Parents will most likely hear them as an invitation to continue on a topic or in a vein the teacher finds useful.

For some parents, their mere presence at a conference plus listening to what teachers report represents a tremendous effort. This effort needs to be acknowledged in ways such as:

> "I sometimes wonder whether I would manage to come to my child's school if things were as difficult for me as I know they are for you."
>
> "It must be hard to come to school when so often what you hear is difficult to listen to."

For the parent who must deal with painful material:

> "I know this is very difficult (or hard for you) to talk about and I admire your courage in staying with it."

d. *Supportive comments to parents who experience difficulties in raising their youngsters*

Parents who are having a hard time raising their youngsters can be helped by knowing they are not alone in their difficulties. Comments which tell parents we do not consider them inadequate are:

> "Join the club."
>
> "We all have 20:20 hindsight."
>
> "Don't we wish we had all the answers all the time."
>
> "Many parents have the same feelings."

Such comments also can prevent the conference from slipping into a discussion of help-lessness or pity or about "what ought to have been done." Following the supportive comment with a statement such as, "Let's see what we can put together about _____," directs the conference to what needs to be explored or what plans need to be worked out *for the present situation.*

e. *Comments that help keep the conference in focus*

At times, what the parent says seems unrelated to the discussion. Comments such as the following help to refocus the conference:

"Help me to know how (what the parent said) is tied up with _____?"

"I'm not sure how that fits. We were discussing _____."

"Would you tell me more about _____ (the last point of the discussion before things got hazy)."

"What you said before about _____ seems important. Would you tell me some more?"

"We both got off the track. We were thinking (or talking) about _____."

Keeping the conference focused is the responsibility of the teacher. Going off on tangents may at times bring momentary relief but it does not accomplish the business for which parent and teacher have met.

4. *Emotionally laden statements—"Red Flags"*

a. "Name calling" or labeling.

Some words are communication stoppers because they seem to "name call" or label student behavior. Name-calling words are usually adjectives which categorize many different behaviors. While occasionally they are useful as "professional shorthand" they are imprecise in common usage.

Would all of us have the same mental picture of a student who is *hyperactive, immature, aggressive, undisciplined, attention-seeking, lazy, unfocused, shy, disruptive, hostile, socially isolated, manipulative?*

Name-calling adjectives often are used as if they explain behavior and can give us clues about how to help youngsters learn more effective behaviors. Saying "(S)he does that because (s)he's lazy" simply states how we have categorized that youngster. It doesn't explain anything nor does it tell us what to do to help. *Lazy* is just a way (and a dismissing one) of saying, "(S)he doesn't do work that should be done." The same child may not be at all lazy on the playground, in art, playing the guitar, or executing intricate plans for mischief.

To say a child is *shy* is not an explanation of why (s)he has no friends. It is the name of a category containing several behaviors (not talking, hanging back, blushing, not volunteering). People who lack friends may be shy, or they may be many other things. Also, many shy people have lots of friends.

If a youngster is labeled *hyperactive*, it usually means (s)he is less quiet than those around would like. To call a youngster *immature* says that the adults wish (s)he would do more often what *they* want. But it says it in a way which not only labels that child as inadequate but doesn't help to correct the situation.

Name calling also interferes with communication because it can frighten or anger parents. When parents hear that their youngster is "immature," "manipulative," "unfocused," etc., they may translate these words into: "The teacher sees my child as inadequate," or "My child gives the teacher a lot of trouble," or "My child is a danger to him/herself and others," or "The teacher thinks I have not done well by my child and expects me to do something so my child behaves differently."

Even when teachers conscientiously avoid labeling students, parents may label them, with a statement that sounds as if it explains the youngster's behavior. "(S)he's just lazy," says mother, or "(S)he just does that because (s)he wants attention." We need to say to such parents: "Some people describe youngsters who rarely turn in their homework as lazy, but I don't like to use words like that because they don't help me know how we can best help your child work harder to do things which still are difficult." Or, "Yes, (s)he now gets attention by doing things which make other kids laugh. But (s)he can learn to get the attention (s)he wants by doing increasingly better work and being a good classmate. That's what we need to think about—how (s)he can learn to get attention for things that are helpful to him/her."

b. *Words as polarizing symbols.*

Words sometimes become symbols or beliefs or behaviors around which attitudes become polarized into "for" or "against." *Permissiveness, open-education, behavior modification, humanism* may be such symbols. If we find a particular word affects us or a parent in a polarizing way, we need to avoid that word.

We have taught many parents the value of letting their children know when they do things well and parents are pleased. We have found it often pays to use words such as *acknowledge, praise, affirm, value,* rather than using the term *positive reinforcement.* Some parents and some teachers respond to *strokes* while others would prefer *praise.*

Problem is a word which acts as a polarizing symbol pushing some parents into a "does (s)he or doesn't (s)he" dilemma. Consequently, we often avoid using the word *problem* because of its potential negative impact, especially for parents who have an inner readiness to hear dire news.

There are times, however, when we need to say to parents in unambiguous terms: "We have a problem." Raising or lowering parents' concern in order to increase their motivation for productive action follows the same principles that the teacher uses to increase students' motivation in the classroom.

Sometimes, when we are describing a typical behavior or a common educational need, such as youngsters having to learn how to solve conflicts with peers or how to approach a new task with confidence, the parent may react by anxiously asking: "Does (s)he have a problem?" or "Is (s)he a problem?" When this happens, conference time may have to be spent on "is or isn't this a problem" or on needing to reassure the parent so that the feelings aroused are not counterproductive.

To avoid getting an unintended parental reaction of "Oh dear, (s)he has a problem," the following is useful:

(1) We tell the parent at the beginning of the conference that the student has no serious problems. We will be describing growth and strengths as well as areas where additional growth is needed. When speaking about the latter, we identify it as normal for students of this age (if it really is, but we don't white-wash).

(2) We preface the description of the student's lack or lag by a warning such as, "Don't think that what I'm going to say means your child has a problem or isn't doing well. I am merely identifying what (s)he next needs to learn."

(3) We use enabling invitational phrases described in the previous section to involve the parent in an active partnership to encourage student growth.

In summary, the hallmark of skillful communication is the teacher's ability to use language that can be accurately translated both as to word meanings and the context in which those words are used. Facilitating that communication with enabling statements and avoiding emotionally laden words and phrases will do much to enhance the communication process and augment a good relationship between home and school.

THE CHECK-BACK

"I explained it and I thought they understood, but I found out they didn't!"

Assuming that we understand or are understood without checking to make sure this is so, explains some of our human conflicts and failures in personal relationships. Even highly skilled communicators often have difficulties grasping immediately what the other person means.

Therefore, at the beginning of a conference, we introduce the notion that we are after maximum understanding by telling parents to stop us if anything we say isn't clear.

To make sure we understand what the parent says to us and to model the check-back process, we use statements such as, "Let me make sure I understand," or, "Let me check out whether I'm hearing you correctly." Then we rephrase what we heard, continuing the checking process until the parent expresses satisfaction with our restatement.

Examples:

"I want to be sure I hear you correctly. When you say you want Jim really pushed, do you mean you want him to be encouraged to do more or do you want him to be given harder assignments with unpleasant consequences if he doesn't complete them?"

"Then, as you see it, things are. . . ."

If the parent says "No, that isn't what I meant," we stimulate clarification by: "Then help me to understand," which encourages the parent to state the message in a different way.

We also use the check-back to make sure *we* have been understood. Check-back questions which will encourage the parent to tell what (s)he heard us say are:

"Have you noticed _____ also?"

"Am I describing something about _____ which sounds familiar to you (or that you recognize)?"

"Do you have the same impression of _____?"

"I want to check that I've said what I mean. Can you tell me what has come across?"

"Now that we've talked, would you tell me how you see _____?"

"Let's summarize what I've told you about _____ so that I know I've been able to give you a clear picture."

If it becomes evident that the parent does not understand something, we modify our words in the same way we modify a lesson when a student does not understand. "I don't mean Paula is not bright enough to do factoring. I mean, before she can be successful, we have to build in some of the math skills she has not yet mastered."

Summarizing the main points of a conference with the parent and jotting down those points with a carbon copy is an excellent check-back technique. An added dividend is that each participant has a written record. This also becomes a reminder of the decisions or agreements made about what the school, the home and the student are going to do. A summary letter also can serve as a check-back (see pages 98–101).

It is equally important to check the meaning we assign to nonverbal messages and make sure that we interpret gestures, expressions or movements correctly.

One teacher could not make sense of the teary-eyed demeanor of a parent. She said: "You look tearful. Is it something we talked about?" "It's just my new contact lenses," responded the parent. The teacher then could comfortably go on with the conference.

Checks such as the following can help clarify the meaning of a nonverbal message:

"Just now you looked troubled. Am I reading you correctly?"

"You look as if something might be difficult. I wonder if you are uncomfortable talking about this?"

"You pursed your lips as if you just thought of something."

In addition to increasing understanding, the check-back can increase focused listening. If a person needs to repeat something to the speaker's satisfaction, (s)he is more apt to pay attention and attempt to understand what is said rather than to think only about formulating a reply. Checking also indicates valuing the contributions of each participant in the communication by the implication: "I care enough about you to want to understand. I'll work towards that goal until we're both satisfied I've done the best I can."

CLOSING THE CONFERENCE

Whatever has been said, listened to and agreed upon needs to be wrapped up in a few sentences at the end of the conference so that it can be "taken away." Recorded agreements cement relationships and avoid fall-out from decisions reached and information given or received which otherwise might be lost in the multitude of daily tasks. In addition, a statement as to "when we will meet again" builds a bridge to the next conference.

Summarizing the Conference

In reporting conferences, many teachers give parents a copy of a previously written statement which briefly summarizes the information about the student's academic, social and emotional accomplishments. The original becomes part of the student's official record.

If there is no written summary, verbal highlighting of the main points of the conference will suffice. "We see Sally as strong in all academic areas. Things come so easily to her that she doesn't have to work hard to do well. We will concentrate on her working in greater depth to extend her thinking skills. You seem to have no concerns about her as a learner and neither do we." The teacher also would summarize, in one or two sentences, what had been discussed about the student's social and emotional status.

Information getting conferences usually do not end with a written summary but with verbal acknowledgement of and appreciation for information given by the parent. If no useful information emerged, we acknowledge that fact with a statement such as, "We didn't come up with anything really promising today. Let's both keep looking at and thinking about the situation until something occurs to one of us."

Problem solving conferences often are best summarized jointly with the teacher recording (with carbon) the main points on which agreements were reached (see *Chapter 10*). One copy remains at school and the parent retains the other. In complicated or touchy situations, a subsequent summary letter, mailed to the home, (with the school retaining a copy) constitutes an official record for home and school. (See pages 98–101.)

Bridging to the Future

Regularly scheduled conferences need no bridging other than a reminder such as, "I'll look forward to seeing you again at the end of the year," or "Julia's next teacher will enjoy working with you." Most teachers invite parents to get in touch with them should there be any questions and express the expectation that parents will be willing to be called by the teacher should there be a need before the next scheduled conference. Some conferences will end by scheduling an appointment to meet again to look at a specific aspect of student functioning, or perhaps to discuss in more detail an objective which had not been taken up because of lack of time.

At times, specific needs for follow-up arise. An agreement may be made for the teacher to phone the parent at a specified time to check on the success of a plan. Or, the teacher may ask the parent to send a note to school to say how plans are working out. In other cases, a follow-up conference will be scheduled a week or two later to evaluate what has happened in the interim and to make further plans. The decision also might be to wait a while to see how things are going and then determine whether to get together again.

Each participant should leave a conference knowing what has been accomplished, what still needs to be done, to whom responsibilities are assigned and when teacher and parent will meet again.

The teacher's gracious acknowledgement of the parents' contributions to the conference will add warmth to the good-bye.

JUDGING THE SUCCESS OF A CONFERENCE

What happens with the student on subsequent days or weeks, is the only one sure way to measure parent conference effectiveness. Will the parents retain what they heard? Will father's reading with Johnny each evening be productive? Will parents acknowledge and reinforce more appropriate school behaviors? Will information parents gave us about their child really be useful to us in working more productively?

Negative parent responses such as, "That's certainly not the way my child acts at home," or a parent who seems withdrawn, angry or stuck on the "Yes, but _____" record, alert us to possible lack of conference success. Pleasure or acceptance by parents during the conference, however, are not a guarantee of success. Some parents, by their attitude and manner, seem to accept the information we give and actively participate in formulating a plan which promises to be productive. They may even tell others how useful it was to have had the conference. And then, *nothing happens!*

We seem to have been so "brilliant" only to find that some parents do not follow through on what has been agreed upon (just as at times we seem to teach "brilliantly" only our students "don't get it"). There may be some comfort in the fact that at other times when we feel we've failed, we find that the outcomes were productive.

After some conferences, with 20:20 hindsight, we may scold ourselves by thinking,

> "Why didn't I say _____?"
>
> "*Now* I know what (s)he was driving at!"
>
> "I really missed the mark by _____."

After the impact of the interchange with another person has worn off enough to let us reflect on what happened, new ideas, questions and insights emerge. Those hindsights are experienced by the most skilled and thoughtful professionals. We need to remind ourselves of this as we lament lost opportunities and experience the "if I had only" syndrome.

When we feel that things did not go well in the conference, there are still possibilities we can realize.

1. If we have some new insights, we need not feel that we missed the only possible opportunity and thus have irrevocably failed. We can communicate those new ideas or perceptions to parents by phoning them or by writing a note, often with surprisingly positive results.

2. We can plan for a different school person to conference with the parent. Sometimes one person fails in an endeavor and the next person succeeds. Differences in personal styles, skills, position in the school system (the principal's authority, nurse's, counsellor's, psychologist's or social worker's distance from the classroom) might be the difference essential to conference success.

3. We can "abandon ship" for the present. Some parents may have demonstrated time and time again that no amount of conferencing is effective nor does it matter who does the conferencing. The best thing is not to continue to "beat our heads against a stone wall" but rather to concentrate on what we, at school, can do directly with the student. At a future time a different approach may yield better results.

We evaluate success in teaching by observing desirable changes in learning and behavior of students. Our subsequent teaching plans reflect the knowledge gained from that evaluation. These same evaluative clues will enable us to judge the success of parent conferences and incorporate that information in subsequent team work with parents.

Section III   COMMUNICATION THEORY

13. COMMUNICATION
    Will theory help? 49

14. EMOTIONS AFFECT COMMUNICATION
    Watch out—it's hot! 51

15. VALUES AFFECT COMMUNICATION
    Watch out—it's loaded! 55

COMMUNICATION

Humans' highly developed ability to transmit specific knowledge, actions and feelings separates them from all other living organisms. An animal may signal danger by a movement, scent or sound. A human, through words, can make that message very specific: "Watch out for the fourth step from the top, it's very slippery." While an animal can convey the notion that food is available, a human can specify, "Dinner will be ready promptly at six. We're having prime rib, so if you are late it will not be as rare as you like it."

With this highly developed language system augmenting and making nonverbal messages (happiness, fatigue, sorrow, anger) more precise, humans have the greatest potential for accurate, productive and *artistic* communication. This potential, however, is not always realized.

Communication is defined as "making common." To the degree that commonality of perception of what is "meant" occurs, communication is successful. Otherwise it is not, regardless of how many hours are spent in close proximity or how many words have left the lips of the participants.

Communication theoreticians identify *senders* who speak and use body language such as facial expressions, stance, or gestures to send a *message* which conveys an idea or mind picture. *Receivers* take in that message by looking, listening and feeling, then assign meaning to what was perceived.

Words, body language, or actions are used in face-to-face encounters. Other methods of communication, writing, pictures, records, videotapes or films, can bridge barriers of time and space. There are "vibes," telepathy or extrasensory perception (ESP), which surely exist, but as yet are not within the span of control of systematic teaching and learning.

In direct face-to-face or telephone communication, unlike indirect written, or taped communication, the senders and receivers of messages are in constant cyclical flow of interaction. While a speaker is sending messages, (s)he is receiving messages from the listener's facial expression (an expressionless face also conveys a definite message), body language, or voice quality even when the response involves ignoring the message. For the sake of clarity we speak of sending and receiving messages as if they occur discretely, but the constant resonance from the flow of communicative interactions needs to be kept in mind.

The sender, who originates purposeful communication performs four functions. (S)he:

1. Clarifies the message in his/her own mind (not always an easy task).

2. Encodes (translates) the message into language, verbal and nonverbal, which is potentially meaning bearing for the receiver and which will have the likelihood of piercing the receiver's personal filter of emotions, values, beliefs.

3. Checks his/her own personal filter of emotions, values and beliefs so the message can be related without unintended additions or distortions.

4. Monitors the reception of the message for signs of accurate or inaccurate perception. Although it is the receiver's responsibility to "understand" the message, it is the sender's responsibility to maximize the probability that this will happen.

Once the four above functions have been completed, the sender has *no more control over the message*, but becomes an interpreter of the receiver's reactions. If changes, modifications or embellishments are indicated, those adjustments can be made only by subsequent messages.

To complete the process of communication, there must be a receiver who:

1. Decodes (distills) the message from the perceptions of his/her eyes and ears and possibly extrasensory perception.

2. Examines the message for additions or distortions from his/her own personal filters (emotions, values, beliefs).

3. Assigns significance to that message on the basis of his/her previous knowledge and experience.

4. Determines reflectively (by thinking) or reflexively (automatically) a verbal or nonverbal response. Ignoring the message, whether it is done deliberately or not, it also a response.

If communication is not terminated, the receiver then becomes the new sender and, in responding, assumes the four sender functions. The sender of the original message becomes the receiver of the subsequent message and assumes receiver responsibilities.

It is important to remember that these same functions exist in non-face-to-face communication. However, the immediate resonance of communicative interaction, with its potential for modifying or correcting the message between sender and receiver, may not be possible.

While communicative functions do not necessarily occur as separate steps nor does each function always occur at a conscious level, by considering each one separately we may avoid "shortouts" or "breakdowns" and more nearly achieve the full potential of each step in the communication process. That potential is directly affected by the awareness, sensitivity and skill of both parties in the interaction.

"Who has time to consider all of these aspects of communication?" we, as overworked teachers, ask. The answer is, "No one, unless those skills have been identified and practiced so they become internalized."

As we become increasingly aware of the complexity and potential of successful communication and practice the skills identified in this book, that internalization process will occur.

Watch out—it's hot!

EMOTIONS EFFECT COMMUNICATION

Educators are becoming increasingly aware of the part that emotions play in learning and that the emotional "temperature" of any situation is a crucial component in what is likely to happen.

Parent conferences are no different. Two people come together, each with important emotional strengths and vulnerabilities. The jobs of parenting and teaching are exacting, demanding, subject to high visibility and consequent potential vulnerability. Success or failure of the adult may seem to be revealed by the performance of the student, someone dear to the parent, important to the teacher, and crucial to society. No wonder when things go well we all feel we can be congratulated and when things don't go well, the atmosphere is charged.

Because teachers, as the professionals, have the major responsibility to see that the emotional charge results in productive activity rather than blackouts or blowups, in a book on parent conferencing it is important that we take a look at the possible impact of the emotional assets and liabilities of the participants in the communication.

Three sources generate a person's emotional state at any particular moment. One, the result of past learning and perhaps genetic or organic predispositions, is the *characteristic emotional state* which pervades a person's being (i.e. typically happy, inquisitive, sure of self, or apprehensive, pessimistic, unsure, or any combination of these with a myriad of other traits).

A second source is the person's *temporary emotional state* which is the result of the *present situation* (i.e. tired, ill, angry, annoyed, hungry, satisfied, pleased, scared, etc.).

The third source of a person's emotional state is the *relationship of the present situation to his/her value system*, resulting in feelings of either acceptance or rejection.

All three of these emotional fountainheads exert influence on both parent and teacher. Consequently, all of them affect the climate of a parent-teacher conference. So we may deal productively with whatever climate exists, we need to examine each source but with full knowledge that a person's emotional state at any particular moment is the result of complex interactions between all three sources.

We will consider first the characteristic emotional state, the way a person typically perceives his/her own reality and the reality of the environment. Then we will examine the modifications which a current situation may bring to the more pervasive state. In the following chapter we will discuss the values which are held by a person and how confirmation of or interference with those values exerts a powerful effect on perceptions and emotions. If it becomes apparent that there is a communication barrier between teacher and parent because each subscribe to different value positions, there are things we can do.

1. *Characteristic Emotional State*

Experience, with feedback from significant others in our lives, has led us to conclude that we occupy positions on many continua which extend from being liked to being disliked, attractive to unattractive, competent to incompetent, sought after to rejected, intelligent to dumb, lucky to unlucky, being in charge of our destiny to destiny being in charge of us.

From this complex matrix of experiencing both the events of our lives and the signals about us sent by significant others, emerges our notion of ourselves which, learned from our past, we then use as a predictor of our future. We perceive reality in terms of our experience-based guess of what will probably happen. "I'll get another poor report on my child," vs. "I'll hear good things about my child," or "Another parent who won't be satisfied, vs. "Parents will work cooperatively with me."

Parents and teachers bring their unique, experience-based emotional "sets" to each conference. Two such sets which can become barriers to communication are brought by parents, *because they are parents.* These sets are:

a. *Their experiences as students.*

A parent's *own childhood experience as a student* can exert a powerful influence on the mood in which that parent comes to the conference.

Parents have been children in school. Some come to a conference with memories of a happy, successful school life. Some bring appreciation of the privilege of schooling accorded their child even though it may have been denied to them. Others may have unhappy memories of frustration from their schooling. This can be true even for the very bright and/or very successful parents who may have found school a dull, irrational (to them), demanding place. Parents who felt impotent, afraid or angry when they were school children may, even though they are not little and helpless in the present, reactivate in themselves those painful childhood feelings through contact with schools.

b. *The feelings generated by their child's performance.*

Parental emotions can also be aroused by the fact that the result of successful or unsuccessful parenting is highly visible at school. Children are the Achilles' heel for many parents and constitute a spot where there is great vulnerability. Therefore, many parents *rate themselves* by their children's school performances. A child doing well at school gives pleasure as a validation of good parenting and may serve as a measure of the parents' own adequacy. Consequently, many parents feel that *they* are being evaluated when their youngster's school performance is described to them. A statement such as, "Johnny is a pleasure to have in my classroom" (which does not say much about Johnny as a learner) may mean to parents that they have been "good" and received an "A." If less than an "A" in parenting is suggested by the school report, parents may deny that anything is less than perfect, as if they could not bear the implication.

Other parents seemingly cannot accept good reports about their children. For whatever reason (perhaps their characteristic emotional state is to believe themselves incapable or unworthy of having a child performing well or being well-liked), they reject seeing their child in positive terms, as if to say, "We know there is nothing all right about us, therefore, there can't be anything all right about our child."

Whenever parents consistently interpret their child's performances differently from the teacher, whether it is that the child must do well to bolster the parents' own self-value or that the child could not do well to reaffirm the parents' lack of self-value, an interference to productive communication occurs.

At those times we need to recognize that parental behaviors which seem troublesome and irrational to us may be self-protective responses and the best that person has figured out to do.

We cannot expect to have major impact on a parent's characteristic emotional state but we can be sensitive to it. If a parent who comes to a conference feeling helpless or scared (note: the word is *feels* not *is*), is invited and encouraged to feel more worthwhile because (s)he is contributing in important ways, (s)he may be willing to see him/herself as more adequate to the task at hand. This may lessen the effect of old feelings in the present situation.

If, in the conference, we find that our perceptions of a student differ from the parent's, we can openly confront that fact and thereby invite the parent to entertain the idea that his/her impression of the child is not the only one possible. We can say: "I know that you feel your child could not possibly be involved in such a situation (or could not be spending time in such manner, or, is not challenged by assignments), but I see it differently," or, "I know your experience with your child is that often (s)he doesn't do things that please you, but here in school I'm very pleased."

Teachers also have experienced-based emotional sets which may become barriers to communication. Two sets are:

a. *Experiences with their own parents.*

All of us have, at times, been disappointed in our parents and been a disappointment to them. As a result, some of us carry past feelings of guilt or anger into the present. Those feelings, unrecognized, can interfere with our actions.

If, through self-examination, we find that we frequently bristle, are angry, or unduly disappointed when a parent lets one of our students down, we may be reacting with "throw-back" feelings to our own childhood when we were disappointed that our own parents were not more helpful, loving, or omnipotent. If, on the other hand, we find that, in difficult situations, we usually focus on parents' pain and disappointments, we may be overly identifying with parents and, as a result, be too protective of their feelings and not be decisive and explicit in statements to them. We may even not ask of them what they can realistically contribute to the conference or to their child's learning.

b. *Experiences as students.*

Teachers, like parents, also have memories of how it felt to be a school child. For some, school is remembered as a benign and enabling experience; for others, school was a harsh, demanding environment. Having made it up the educational ladder is no guarantee against painful memories.

If through self-examination we find that we frequently don't hold students responsible for their own learning and behavior, but instead blame "the system," the past, or ourselves, we may be over-identifying with students. On the other hand, if we seldom recognize that students and their parents have needs, wishes, and rights which can be violated by "the system" and society, we may be overly identifying with "the system."

The important thing to remember is that each of us has a history which influences our ways of perceiving and acting in the present. We need to be alert to the influence of the past and ask ourselves: "Am I seeing what is going on *now*, or am I reacting to memories of my own childhood?" Unchecked, those memories can become barriers to communication.

2. *Temporary Emotional State*

Even the most amiable of us, at times, is driven to exasperation, the most despairing can have hopes raised, and the most truculent become quiet. Current circumstances of high intensity have the power to temporarily change a characteristic emotional stance. The most common change is one we experience with a pleasant surprise, unexpected good luck, sudden illness, pain, hunger, fatigue or an unanticipated situation. Parents can experience a disquieting temporary change in mood when their child announces, "I got into trouble at school today." In the same way, teachers may experience a change in mood when a student states, "My father says he is coming to school to observe."

Parents may come to a conference hassled, with physical pain, good or bad news unrelated to school, or a host of other problems. At times, they share with us how they feel at the beginning of a conference. At times, they do not.

We often become aware of the mood of others through their nonverbal messages. If we suspect that a parent's temporary emotional state may interfere with communication, it is best to check this out: "Are you under pressure today?" "Did you have a hard time getting here?" "Often it is difficult for parents to make the time to come for these conferences." If said with empathy, often the parent will relax, perhaps briefly share feelings and, having been acknowledged, participate more freely in the conference.

Our own characteristic emotional state may also be modified or intensified by the day we have had. If it was a rainy, noisy day, if our carefully made plans didn't work out well, if this is the day of our evaluation conference with the principal, we may not be at our best. On the other hand, if we have just heard about the salary increase, if our students have behaved like angels all day or if we've just received an "outstanding" rating by the principal, we may temporarily not be nearly so concerned about a student's reluctance to finish work. Consequently, the way we report to the parent, ask for information, or approach him/her to collaborate with us in a problem-solving session may differ as a result of our own current mood.

We need to be aware when our temporary emotional state beclouds our perceptions or interferes with our performance and use our good sense and sensitivity to correct for our mood in order to give the best service possible to our clients.

It would be presumptuous to imply that the authors could do more than indicate the importance of characteristic and temporary emotions to communication. Awareness is, however, a first step toward mastery of any skill. Awareness of the impact of emotions to communication is no different.

VALUES EFFECT COMMUNICATION

Communication is at best difficult, and, at worst, impossible for people whose values are very different. Because value positions can become a barrier in parent conferences, differences must be taken into account so acknowledgement or resolution of those differences can be achieved.

Parents and teachers may not hold the same values. What makes for a "good child" can be different for school and home. If the parent values *only* academic achievement and the teacher feels social adjustment is equally important, interference in communication is predictable. If a parent values a child doing as (s)he is told, and the teacher values independent decision making, communication may be jammed by this divergence. We've had a mother ask us in amazement, "Don't you want children to do what they are told?" when she heard her kindergartner needed to learn to make choices on his own.

Some parents value children who are seen and not heard. Teachers, however, might perceive a student's reluctance to express him/herself as burdensome and provide opportunities where the child could feel free to assert an opinion. Some parents feel that schools are too restrictive and value more autonomy for their children while teachers may feel there is not enough respect for the rights of others.

Similar events often are interpreted differently by people with different values. To one young mother, her values regarding housekeeping and child raising were sound. To the grandmother, the house seemed a shambles and the time spent on going bicycling with the children or taking them to museums and concerts, a waste of energy and money.

Openness about feelings may mean desirable authenticity and a sign of good mental health to one person or an uncomfortable lack of decorum and a vulgar self-indulgence to another. A student's behavior may be interpreted as that of a model obedient child *or* as seriously lacking in self-assertiveness. To different people, the noise level in a classroom may mean that the children are productively interacting or that they are noisily wasting time.

Values are those beliefs that influence our perceptions, the meanings and importance we assign to those perceptions, and our resultant behaviors. Values guide us in the decisions about what matters and what doesn't, what we will exert effort to achieve and what we believe is not worth the effort.

Values may be considered ultimate truths by one group or society, but not by others. Within each group or society there is general acceptance of some basic values, and great divergence in acceptance of others.

It is important to emphasize that a *value*, as the term is used here, is neither right nor wrong. It is a preference. Each of us develops a value system which reflects both personal and societal values and forms the framework from which we act.

To work productively with someone whose values may differ from ours, it is important that we base our actions on acknowledgement of the following:

1. Values are learned.
2. Values are ranked in importance.
3. Values of similar rank may compete with each other.
4. Values can be modified or changed.

1. *Values Are Learned.*

From parental examples and responses to their infant's behaviors, a child learns what to pay attention to and what is *important, good, correct, bad,* etc. If the child adapts to the parent's values, (s)he is rewarded by feeling accepted. In time, the child internalizes what has been rewarded and believes that it is the way "I should be" and the way "things should be." Later, the child discovers that other people may have different ideas about what is *good, bad, correct, important.* The child may adopt some values of people and groups which have become important and modify or reject some previously held values. Again, the child is rewarded with acceptance by those whose values (s)he adopts.

From a child's experiences and from the values of significant others is welded the value system by which that child lives. A value system may continue to be modified or may remain the same depending on future learning and experience.

2. *Values Are Ranked in Importance.*

Values range from those of little importance (those of slight preference), through somewhat important values (those about which we have stronger feelings), to those of great importance (those we would fight to keep), to centrally crucial values (those which have become so vitally important that changing them would mean changing our whole perception of ourselves and the world).

3. *Values of Similar Rank May Compete with Each Other.*

While we may, at times, experience difficulties in obeying the dictates of our conscience, we do not experience inner conflicts about it. We can, however, experience conflicts about values of equal or near equal rank. We want children to work hard to achieve; we also want them to have fun. We want students to be self-directed, but we want them to do what we believe they ought to do. Love of mother and love of wife, love of spouse and love of child, meeting one's own needs and being considerate of others, are typical values which can conflict with each other.

A parent may not want a child to be physically aggressive, yet want the child to defend him/herself; or may want a child to be a good student, yet be popular and not an "intellectual;" or may wish to develop the child's independence, yet wish to protect the child.

A teacher may stress the use of appropriate language yet also believe that students should let others know their feelings which could, at first, result in the use of language that was not so appropriate. A teacher may want a student to work carefully yet to get finished with the work in the allotted time.

Competing values within a person can cause emotional static. Should two values become antithetical in a particular situation, one value must take precedence; we can't have both so we must settle for one *or* the other.

4. *Values Can Be Changed.*

Since values are learned, they can be modified by new learning. The ease with which that modification occurs depends on three factors:

a. *How centrally important is this value to the person's maintenance of self and view of the world?* To alter a central value may imply, "My life so far has been based on a huge mistake," and therefore, that value may not be subject to modification.

This could be the reason some parents do not change their perceptions of their child no matter how many experts suggest they do so. Perhaps their need to hold onto beliefs that their child is a certain kind of person is a central value and, to all intents and purposes the belief is not modifiable.

Academic performance may be a central value to a parent as the only way to the good life. Consequently, when a teacher tries to communicate that academic learning is very difficult for the child, but that (s)he is fascinated by machinery and is unusually skilled at fixing things, the parent may be unable to hear, much less accept the message because it is so threatening to that which is crucially important.

b. *Has the person had experiences that have the potential to modify a value?* The possiblity for change in values occurs when we are exposed to *significant* people, information, or ideas that present values different from our own. The immigrant, exposed to a new culture with its different values, may adopt those values. The youngster going to school for the first time may be exposed to different values of significant others. An over-protective mother may be exposed to the value of her child's independence in school learning. A culturally disadvantaged child, entering school, may be exposed to a world of people who value books and that child may begin to value reading (part of the effect of Headstart).

Parents of a young child may see only the individual needs of their child, and may not perceive the needs and rights of other youngsters in the classrooms. Should these parents have the experience of becoming school aides, volunteers or youth group leaders, they will gain new knowledge and with it, perhaps, new values. Then perceptions of what *should be* for their own children and others, also may change.

The difference between a person who is *uninformed* and a person whose *values* will not permit the intake of new information, is that the former will more readily incorporate the new information into his/her value system.

c. *If new values are accepted, will this be perceived as a rewarding experience?* Originally, all of us learned what to value because we were rewarded for doing so by feeling accepted by those who cared for us, and because we were punished directly or by nonacceptance if we did not comply. Consequently, it has to be worthwhile for us to change a value, whether the reward is from others or from feeling good about the change.

Whenever people change, it is for reasons important to them: greater acceptability, a sense of increased self-worth, because something just makes more sense or gives a greater sense of fulfillment. The payoff to parents for modification of values is the improved functioning of the child as reported with enthusiasm by the teacher. Sensitivity to the need for reinforcing a parent's attempts to incorporate a new value may markedly increase the chances of this happening. Consequently, it is essential that the parent be given evidence of the beneficial results from changes the parent has made.

What Can Be Done When There Are Value Differences Between Home and School?

After the parent has been given information and it becomes clear that there are different values operating between home and school, it is possible to avoid an impasse through *value ranking*. Our task then becomes the identification of which value has priority for the parent by looking at the possible consequence of the decision made on the basis of the conflicting values. Parents are entitled to valid, nonjudgemental *information* about the child's performance at school and the consequences. Our job is to describe what the child *does or does not do*, avoiding statements about what the child *is*. "Suzie has not yet learned to take turns, so she was not chosen as a team member," rather than, "Suzie is selfish." "When he is angry, Bill uses words that are not acceptable at school and many of the children avoid him," rather than, "Bill is rude." In this way, we are providing the new nonjudgemental experience or information.

A father was told that his son was defiant of all school rules, ran out of the room, and as a result, had little time for academic learning. At first, the father supported his son, feeling that defiance of authority showed the boy had a strong ego, and that the boy needed to learn to withstand institutionalized pressures which could stifle his independence. However, the father also wanted the boy to be well educated. In the conference, he was helped to see the educational consequences of the boy's behaviors. Upon reflection, the father then ranked the value of "not buckling under authority" below that of academic learning and began to support the school rather than his son's defiance. Subsequently, the boy made progress.

The mother of a kindergarten girl valued not hampering her child's free verbal expressions with the result that the girl's language was so inappropriate that other parents would not let their children play with her. The mother then became concerned about the girl's lack of friends and decided that the value of free use of language ranked below the value of making and holding friends and subsequently helped the teacher to eliminate the inappropriate language. As a result, mother and child felt good about the girl's having friends—a validation of her improved functioning.

If a mother learns that protecting her child too much has detrimental effects, she may begin to rank the value of "protection" below that of "independence."

Why Identify Value Differences?

A final question to be considered is: Why might we wish to express our values if we know or suspect that a parent has different ones? The answer is: there is always a possibility of change if we say what we believe (just as there is a possibility of our changing if we listen openly to what others believe). There are no such possibilities when we don't.

Expression and consideration of differing values has been labeled *seed throwing*. At times, these seeds take root and grow. At other times, they fall on barren soil. One cannot know the potential of the "soil" on which ideas will fall. Only time will reveal the *full* effects of a parent conference. Some parents, when shown in a conference that their previous beliefs about the youngster were inaccurate, have learned to perceive their child differently and value him/her more. Some parents have learned to accept that their child is bright when they previously thought (s)he was not; others have become aware that their youngster with limited ability is working hard at maximum capacity and valued their child more for putting forth optimum effort.

Finally if having tried, we can't resolve the value differences, we and the parent can *agree not to agree*, but value the other's right to a different opinion.

Holding different values is a fact of life when many people of varied backgrounds live and work together in a pluralistic society such as ours. It is important that in conferencing with parents, we are aware that the values we and the parent hold are based on personal history. We may strongly believe that something a parent values or does is not in the best interest of the child; it may, in fact, be something that offends our value system. Nevertheless, parents have as much right to their values (unless they run counter to the laws of the community) as we have to ours.

Children need not be damaged by the fact that school and home hold different values. It is important that even very young children learn that values can differ and that some actions are appropriate in school and other actions at home, just as they need to learn that there is an indoor voice and outdoor voice. Recognizing that differences in behaviors and values exist without one being right and the other wrong, can be a productive learning opportunity.

Damaging to youngsters is the feeling on the part of home or school that the other's values are "bad" or "wrong" so that the children end up in confusion about what to do to resolve differences in a world where if they behave the way the school wishes, they offend the parents and vice versa.

It is in the best interest of children that home and school work together. Parents and teachers can do so even when they do not hold the same values if they accept and respect the fact and then, agreeing not to agree on their value positions, agree that they will to work together for the benefit of the student.

There are times when the best summary statement of a difference in value positions is: "We do not have the same perceptions or give the same interpretations to what is going on. I respect your stand; hopefully you will respect mine. Now let's both do the best we can for your youngster."

Section IV   SPECIAL CONSIDERATIONS

16. AUGMENTING THE CONFERENCE WITH ADDITIONAL PARTICIPANTS
    Who should be present? 61

17. THE STUDENT'S ROLE IN PARENT CONFERENCES
    What are students' rights and responsibilities? 63

18. THE TELEPHONE CONFERENCE
    Is this a good time to talk? 65

19. CONFIDENTIALITY
    With whom may I share information? 71

AUGMENTING THE CONFERENCE WITH ADDITIONAL PARTICIPANTS

Whenever feasible, both parents should be encouraged to attend conferences so they hear the same message and participate in decisions. This can avoid some of the distortions or omissions that frequently occur when messages are relayed from one person to another or when decisions which affect both parents and their child are agreed to by only one parent. It is also desirable to have both parents attend conferences because communication between home and school is so important in raising and educating a child.

In most routine conferences, the mother will be the only family member and the teacher the only professional present. There are occasions, however, when inclusion of other professional or family participants is desirable.

The parent has the right to suggest augmentation of conference participants. However, the decision as to those present usually is made by the teacher. Guiding that decision is an estimate of whose presence will aid achievement of the conference objective.

Additional participants can contribute to the conference by their:

1. *Knowledge of the student*
Family members, professionals in the school, occasionally other professionals who know the student can contribute important information and insights.

When there is a teaching team, the presence of an additional team member gives a more inclusive picture, lends credence to the report and furthers the development of viable plans for the student. These dividends need to be weighed against the time involved for the second team member.

With parental agreement and sometimes by their request, grandparents or others who are important to the child or who play a major role in child rearing also can be included in the conference.

Inclusion of the student in the conference, as a knowledgeable contributor and to further his/her own learning is so important that the next chapter will deal with that role and the preparation necessary to make participation successful.

2. *Ability to facilitate communications*
A third person representing either home or school sometimes can hear and state ideas more objectively than the parent or teacher, yet give support to both.

3. *Additional expertise or authority*

At times, the need for additional resources, information, or for the authority to finalize decisions makes the inclusion of other professionals or family members useful.

Including another professional in a conference also can serve the important purpose of professional development. Beginning teachers can learn conferencing skills through observation of more experienced staff members. Experienced teachers may ask a colleague to observe them and give feedback and suggestions to improve communication skills. Many parents will, if asked, give permission for another teacher to attend their conference or for videotaping for inservice purposes or as a powerful new way for parents, students and teachers to "see ourselves as others see us."

Whenever either side has augmented its representation, the other side may feel somewhat overwhelmed by a feeling that "there is only me with all these powerful others." Consequently, teachers should inform parents of the intention to include additional school personnel and be sensitive to their reaction. "I've asked the principal to join us because . . . " or "Our counsellor, who has worked with Helen and knows her well, will join us. In that way, we can get some additional ideas of how we might best work." This gives the parent an opportunity to know beforehand that others will be present.

Sometimes, the teacher needs to acknowledge his/her own feelings when a number of family members are present. "It's a new situation for me to meet with several members of your family and I feel a bit overwhelmed."

In summary, the decision to include additional participants in a conference must be based on three considerations: 1) how best to achieve the major objective, 2) the economical use of people's time, and 3) the creation of positive feelings and extension of maximum support to all participants.

THE STUDENT'S ROLE IN PARENT CONFERENCES

Students' participation in parent conferences mirrors today's belief in the rights of all individuals, including minors, to know and be involved in what others say about and plan for them. Instead of merely being passive, talked-about and decided about objects, students are entitled to the right and opportunity to become active, discerning and decision making participants in a process which involves them and their future. They also have the responsibility and opportunity for becoming more objective about their own growth and achievement.

Students increasingly are being invited to take an active part in their own reporting conferences. Teachers, parents, and the students themselves report satisfaction with this involvement. Students also are invited to become active and accountable participants in conferences that are held to make plans to remediate or enrich their performances.

It is an excellent real life learning opportunity for students to take an active part in their own conferences in order that they:

1. Assess and evaluate their own performance. Going through the process of preparing to report their growth gives students the opportunity to reflect on their achievements, preferences and dislikes, strengths and weaknesses, on what they have accomplished well, on what they next need to work. Even very young children can tell about their friends, what they most enjoy and are interested in learning next, and choose work that they want their parents to see or know about.

2. Put facts and ideas about themselves into words that communicate important information.

3. Consider their progress and develop agreed-to plans for action which might contribute to their future growth.

In addition to the opportunity for growth, there are other dividends from students' participation in conferences:

1. The student's presence in a conference enables parents to see their child in new areas of competence and need. This can lend credence to the teacher's description of achievement and classroom behaviors.

2. Students can contribute to parents' understanding of the school and their child's academic and social role in that environment.

3. Because, in the past, schools involved students and their parents in conference only if there was a problem (good kids aren't sent to the counselor or principal, nor do their teachers call in their parents), both students and parents may be conditioned to the idea that the school focuses mainly on the bad, problematic, and troublesome. Including students in their own conferences can alter that attitude by sharing the feelings of success as learning and growing takes place.

Occasionally, there are parents who downgrade their youngsters. If the teacher anticipates that this might occur, the student should not be involved in the conference. Such youngsters are entitled to protection of their dignity and self-respect.

PREPARING STUDENTS TO PARTICIPATE EFFECTIVELY IN CONFERENCES.

Many teachers use questionnaires to help youngsters think about their achievements in preparation for their own parent conference (see page 103).

Also, with teacher guidance, students can identify the information they wish to give their parents as well as accept the responsibility for determining problematic areas in which their parents have interest and the right to information.

A student's eagerness or reluctance to participate, plus seeing a student and parent interact with each other, gives additional information about the parent-child relationship. We need to be responsive to this information. When a student is reluctant to share something which we feel a parent has a right to know, we might say: "It's your choice whether you or I tell your parents about _____." The student's answer helps us determine ways to deal with information the student does not wish to communicate.

GUIDING STUDENTS' PARTICIPATION IN A CONFERENCE.

The basic guiding principle is that students must feel they are participating in a process which dignifies them as worthy persons. To feel not in charge of oneself, put down, or less able as a result of being part of the conference is not an acceptable humanistic or educational goal.

Support for a student can be built around his/her previous planning or the questionnaire (s)he completed. "You mentioned on your form that _____ was hardest for you." After the student presents information, the teacher can elaborate should additional examples or information be indicated.

In the authors' experience, youngsters who initially were reluctant to participate in reporting conferences, became comfortable when they had only one task to perform (perhaps to show a piece of work or to describe the one subject that is easiest or hardest for them). Sometimes, by being assured they need only to listen, youngsters become comfortable in being part of the conference. Sometimes, it also can be appropriate for the student to be present for only part of the conference and then be allowed to leave while the teacher finishes the report. In most cases, the student has a right to know what, in essence, the teacher and the parent discussed after (s)he left. Letting students know their contribution is valued and that they have done a good job in presenting it, goes a long way toward developing feelings of adequacy and comfort in future conferences.

Many teachers have reported that their initial fears that it would be difficult for students to participate in conferences were unfounded. Nervousness existed more on the part of parents and teachers than on the part of students. Adults, whether parents or professionals, are used to "talking about" youngsters. The effort it takes to rethink our "for adults only" conferencing habits, and to try something that involves the student, not only meets today's trend towards acknowledging student rights and autonomy, but yields benefits in increased student responsibility for learning plus more open and productive working relationships between home and school.

64

THE TELEPHONE CONFERENCE

"The teacher is on the phone," was an announcement that in the past signaled serious school problems. Now education has joined other professions in using the telephone as a useful communication tool in non-crisis situations. With increased professional use of the telephone, it is unfortunate that there is such a paucity of studies or writing about the difference in phone vs. face-to-face encounters and the skills a professional needs in order to work effectively by phone.

THE TELEPHONE AS A PRIMARY CONTACT

At times the telephone is the primary means for communication with parents who are unable or unwilling to come to school. Some are ill. Some have no one at home to care for children. Some cannot leave work at the time teachers are available. Some are reluctant to come to school for personal reasons. They may be ashamed that they don't have nice clothes, look battered or for other reasons (see *Chapter 23*). For some it is easier to talk about sensitive issues on the phone than to discuss them face to face. Some just don't keep appointments.

As a result, for certain parents the phone remains the major avenue of contact with their child's school. Others, having learned through initial phone conferences that the school is truly interested in their child and helpful to them as parents, gain the confidence to come to school.

THE TELEPHONE AS A SECONDARY CONTACT

The telephone is also valuable as a means for communication between home and school to share information and as a time saver in follow-up work.

1. *For Positive Communications*

The pleasure parents experience in a call from the teacher saying that their child was noticed for something well done, or was missed when absent, can go a long way to enhance their attitude towards the child, the school, and possibly even themselves. Such contacts have professional integrity and promote good public relations.

2. *For Follow-up Communication*

The phone is an excellent, time saving way to follow-up on the effectiveness on plans developed during a conference. Examples:

"I'll call to see how your talk with Johnny went and what the two of you decided. When would be a good time to phone?"

"Will you call in a few days to let me know how things are going? How about Tuesday afternoon?" (Or "When would be a convenient time?")

"I'll call you on Friday afternoons for the next few weeks and check with you (report to you) on how things have gone."

DIFFERENCES BETWEEN TELEPHONE AND FACE-TO-FACE COMMUNICATION

To use the telephone effectively in professional communication, we need to take into account the following differences:

1. Visual information, present in face-to-face encounters, is absent in a phone interaction. As a result, neither person has available the other's body language which enhances, validates or impeaches the words used.

2. Neither knows the conditions at the other end of the line (children quarreling, dinner burning, relatives present, the carpool ready to leave, or other teachers waiting to use the office phone, the principal waiting to see the teacher).

3. Either person can terminate the communication by hanging up, an action which may be easier than walking out of a room. There is no visual warning that the listener cannot take any more, which in face-to-face communication gives the speaker an opportunity to soften or modify the message in order to help the listener stay with the communication.

4. The degree of control or the power of professionals working in their own office (their profession "turf") may shift when the client (parent) is on the phone in his/her own home or place of work. One survey[1] showed that counselors preferred face-to-face encounters; clients preferred to talk on the phone. Perhaps for some professionals their office acts as their security blanket while for some clients, being in their own home is one.

All of these differences between phone and face-to-face communication imply that an initial phone communication with parents should, if at all possible, be pleasant, be about student growth rather than lack of it, tell what the teacher is doing to help rather than what the parent should do and thereby maximize the possibility of building positive channels of communication which then become available for subsequent team work of parent and teacher.

TELEPHONE MYTHS

Some beliefs about the effectiveness of working professionally via the phone may be myths. There are very few studies comparing the phone with face-to-face communication in counseling, information giving and getting, or in problem solving. More extensive research needs to be done. Studies which exist, however, suggest some surprising answers to the following questions:

1. Do phone encounters result in less client (parent) satisfaction than can be achieved by face-to-face encounters?

Not necessarily. Two recent studies (1) (2) indicate no difference in client satisfaction. Clients perceive empathy, support, and help in problem solving as not being different in phone conferences from office visits.

Experiences in recent years with "warm" and "hot lines" as well as in agencies where people work almost exclusively on the phone also affirm that the phone can be an effective tool in professional work.*

2. Do clients work harder or become more involved when they come to an office than when they are on the phone?

Not necessarily. For many people, the effort it takes to come to an office can deplete energy which otherwise could be available for problem solving. The feelings aroused by having to face another person can be anxiety evoking, especially if that person is felt to have power as a teacher may be felt to have power over parents. Talking on the phone from their own "turf" can help clients feel more secure.

3. Are visual cues crucially important in assessing clients' needs and responses so the professional knows how best to work?

Not necessarily. One study (3) indicated that the most essential channel for communication in problem solving is the voice channel. The addition of a visual channel did not appreciably decrease the time it took to arrive at a solution.

Information gathered from helping professionals who work almonst exclusively on the phone also confirmed that, for them, visual cues are not essential for sensitive assessments of needs, capacity for action and establishment or maintenance of contact.

Elimination of visual cues, which are such an important source of critical information in the classroom, presents a special problem for teachers who, when conferencing by phone, need to learn to understand what is being said without *seeing* what the other person *means*.

INCREASING TELEPHONE SKILLS

To minimize potential problems with "telephone blindness" or discomfort, we can practice the following:

1. *Transfer the Skills Already Known About Face-to-face Communication to Voice-to-Voice Telephone Communication.*

It is important to have a clear objective in mind, to make sure the parent is aware of and agrees to it, to prepare carefully, to employ the same conference skills and evaluation techniques used to achieve a successful face-to-face conference.

---

*We are drawing on information and studies from the field of the helping professions, relating findings in that field to the parent-teacher conference. We are also drawing on our own experiences and on the experiences of others.

Our special thanks go to Sari Reznick and Eleanor D. Grossman of the Information and Referral Service of Los Angeles County, Inc., for their generous contribution of time and for their thoughtful, valuable sharing of experiences and expertise in working professionally almost entirely via the phone.

2. *Develop Analytic Listening Skills.*

In the absence of visual cues, listening skills need to be sharpened. Is the voice quality of the person with whom we are talking relaxed, warm, fluent, or tight, panicky, anxious, flat? Are there hesitations or does the communication flow easily? How the parent breathes may give an indication of a relaxed, comfortable state or a tense, anxious one. Incongruities between the voice quality and the verbal message could indicate that the person does not fully *mean* what the words imply. "It is perfectly all right" said in a tense, uncomfortable voice can indicate that it is *not* all right. Background noises give clues to surroundings at the other end of the telephone—children squabbling, adults talking in the room, doors slamming.

The following will increase sensitivity to auditory signals:
1) Close your eyes and hear the *meaning* of the TV voice.
2) Practice listening without looking at the speaker to become increasingly sensitive to feelings conveyed by auditory cues other than words.
3) Close your eyes and listen to the sounds you hear and infer what information they convey about the surroundings.
4) With parent permission, tape record a face-to-face conference and listen to how you come across.
5) Listen to another teacher's tape recorded conference.

Listening skills, like other skills, are developed by practice. It is amazing how much listening for meaning will increase the ability to *hear* it.

3. *Sharpen Communication Skills.*

In assessing the feelings or attitudes of a parent on the phone, we take into consideration that some parents may not find any conversation with teachers easy. In a face-to-face encounter they can overcome some of their lack of verbal facility with movements such as gestures or shoulder shrugs. On the phone they cannot use these nonverbal assists.

A hesitant voice and halting verbal manner also may signal conditions such as not feeling well, surprise, disbelief, irritation or a host of other emotions.

To avoid making assumptions or being unaware of important factors which are influencing the communication process, we check out with questions or statements the meaning of what we hear. "Am I understanding you correctly that _____?" "Do you mean _____?" "You may wish to think about that and let me know later."

A mother may not feel free to talk because her child, a relative or neighbor just entered the room, not because she wants to avoid a subject.

If we suspect the mother may be busy with a baby, or have another child pulling on her or is in any way preoccupied, we ask, "Are you able to talk freely or would you rather I phone at another time?"

If there is a long silence, we ask questions such as, "You may be thinking about what I've said. Would you like some more information?" "Is there a question you would like to ask?" While waiting for the parent to continue, we give reassurance. "It's O.K. to take some time. I'll wait while you think about it," or use similar remarks.

Because we cannot give visual signs of welcome, warmth, acceptance or reassurance, our repertoire of verbal initiators and enablers is especially important in conveying that it is all right for the parent to grope for words, block, to be uncertain or not understand. "It's O.K." "Take your time." "I'm still here." "That's hard to talk about." "Many people would be at a loss for words." "I'm glad you're taking the time to talk with me." "Do you want to think about that for a few moments?" "Tell me some more about that." "Do you mean _____ or _____?" Saying "uh-huh," "I see," "oh really!" "that's important," will also help the parent know we are interested.

4. *Develop a Gracious Telephone Voice.*

Many of us, unintentionally, sound more abrupt on the phone than we sound when talking face to face. This may have something to do with the mechanics of voice transmissions. It could also be a result of the fact that we typically think of using the phone for brief messages and short conversations rather than to accomplish professional tasks. Therefore, we can feel uncomfortable, hurried and sound abrupt. We need to practice speaking softly and as little clipped as possible. Making a tape recording of our end of a phone conference enables us to hear our strengths and identify skills we wish to improve.

If we say to ourselves, "I'll spend 20 minutes talking with the parent on the phone, which is probably the same amount of time I would spend if (s)he came to see me at school," the hurried feeling may lessen. It is essential to check that the parent also has that same 20 minutes to spend on the phone.

5. *Acknowledge Feelings about Phoning.*

There is a quotient of personal preference for the phone ranging from ease to marked discomfort. Therefore, we need to know our own reactions. If we are a "it's a useful gadget but" person, we may need to acknowledge and adjust for our discomfort lest the parent "hear" our feelings and believe they are directed at him/her. We might say something such as, "I'm never too comfortable speaking on the phone. I tell you that so you won't think it has anything to do with you."

Also, if indicated, we ask the parent how (s)he feels about talking on the phone. Even if, not having previously thought about it, (s)he does not know how to respond, at least there is acknowledgement that feelings towards phone communication exist and those feelings have to be taken into account so they do not become a barrier to communication.

TELEPHONE MANNERS

Telephone manners are based on each participant's rights and responsibilities and are as important as manners in other human interactions.

1. *Parents' Rights.*

The phone is intrusive. It rings and commands those of us who will be so commanded to respond. Therefore, we ask the parent, "Is this a time that is convenient for you?" "Can you talk now or suggest a time that would be better?"

If, in a face-to-face conference, we set follow-up telephone appointments we need to agree on mutually convenient times.

Except for an emergency, we never call a parent at work unless we have previously established that the parent is agreeable to accepting such calls. Many parents have jobs which would be jeopardized if they spent time on personal business. Other parents do not wish co-workers to know of their affairs, especially matters that concern their children in school.

When we call a student's home and someone other than the parent answers the phone, we are careful how we identify ourselves and relay our message. We might say, "It's no problem but I wanted an opportunity to talk with _____. Do you know when it might be a good time to call?" Rather than make an unannounced call, we might write a note indicating our need to talk and ask the parent to suggest a convenient time.

2. *Teachers' Rights.*

The phone can be as intrusive to us as to parents. We need to protect ourselves from phone chores that we cannot comfortably accommodate. We can set aside an early morning or late afternoon hour or two each week to make necessary phone calls.

When we phone to set a time for a subsequent conference, we may feel pushed by parents who, understandably, want to know what the problem is. They may deal with their apprehensions by insisting we tell them "What this is all about."

Unless we and the parent have ample time for discussion, we stipulate at the beginning that it will not be productive to discuss the matter now, we really need to meet together. We might give a very brief statement of the situation such as "I want to talk with you about Bruce's reading so together we can make a plan to help him." Then we need to give the parent an appointment as soon as possible.

If we are heavily scheduled, we don't make the initiating phone call. Should the parent say (s)he cannot come to school, we make a telephone conference appointment, asking the parent to set aside sufficient time at an hour convenient to both of us so we can develop a well thought out plan.

At times it is appropriate to suggest that the parent tap the child's feelings about the subject of concern. At other times we may wish to say to the parent, "Perhaps it would be best if you don't ask your child about this yet but wait until you and I have a chance to determine what it is we need to find out." We must, however, be prepared that the parent, with understandable concern, will ignore our request.

The communication and solution of any educational problem is taxing of professional skill, composure and tact. In situations when we do not meet face to face, the ability to function effectively by telephone goes a long way toward reducing stress and increasing satisfaction. Development of phone communication skills is an attainable and highly desirable objective in professional growth.

NOTES

[1]Antonioni, David; "A Field Study Comparison of Counselor Empathy, Concreteness and Client Self-Exploration in Face-to-Face and Telephone Counseling During First and Second Interview" *Dissertation Abstracts International*, August 1973, Vol. 34, (2–B), p. 866.

[2]Williams, Tim and Douds, John; "The Unique Contribution of Telephone Therapy," *Crisis Intervention and Counseling by Telephone*, Lester, David and Brookopp, Gene W., eds., (Springfield, Ill.: Charles C. Thomas, 1973), pp 80–88.

[3]Weeks, Gerald and Chapanis, Alphonse; "Cooperative vrs Conflictive Problem Solving in Three Tele-Communication Modes," *Perceptual and Motor Skills*, June 1976, Vol. 42, pp 879–917.

With whom may I share information?

CONFIDENTIALITY

Members of helping professions are deeply concerned with confidentiality as a foundation on which trust, necessary for a working relationship between practitioner and client, is built. Unless parents know that what they reveal to us about themselves or their children will remain "private business" and not be indiscriminately broadcasted, the trust necessary to create collaboration in furthering student learning cannot develop. Therefore, by our assurances, but even more by the evidence of our day-by-day practices, parents must know that unless they **agree** to specific disclosures, what they tell us is *strictly confidential.*

In addition, members of helping professions are concerned about confidentiality because new laws and administrative decisions with far reaching implications for practice are being enacted. As a result, many aspects of confidentiality are being reexamined and dealt with in new ways by those who work professionally. In law, medicine, psychiatry, psychology and social work, the tremendous interest and concern in the subject is evidenced by an abundance of workshops and symposia that deal with laws related to invasion of privacy and protection of human rights. We need to examine their implications and take a new, indepth look at the ethics which underlie practice.

Confidentiality has become one of the hottest issues of the day because of societal and technological changes with far reaching consequences for the relationships between those individuals and institutions giving professional services and the clients being served.

Some of the changes are:

1. Consumerism, demands of accountability for the quality of services and third party payment practices, require that, to assess effectiveness, extensive information including personal data about individuals served, be gathered. Many people not involved in direct service to clients are employed in the data-gathering and evaluating process. As a result, more and more people know more and more about other people.

2. Modern technology not only has made vastly increased collections of data possible, but those data are now available forever.

3. Public disenchantment is growing with the former belief that professionals work invariably in the best interest of those they serve (the doctor no longer always "knows best"). People are questioning how professionals use the information they gather.

4. There is increased public awareness that information constitutes power. Those who know about us have the potential to direct and control us.

5. The "Rights" movement, which started in the 1960's, now includes the Right to Privacy. The Family Educational Rights and Privacy Act, enacted by Congress in 1974, expresses the nation's concern about information gathered and kept by institutions of learning. Those records have the potential for far reaching impact on the lives of students and their families. Clients can find out what information is kept and can challenge the accuracy of that information. Therefore, schools must make ethically and legally responsible decisions about data collection and storage.

Conscientious professionals are in agreement with the aims of the various privacy laws because abuses can and do occur in both public and private institutions. However, professionals are equally concerned with the fact that, in order to render quality service over a long period of time as schools must do, information has to be shared with other professionals. If it is illegal and unethical *not* to protect the privacy of clients by sharing information indiscriminately (no one would subscribe to lunch room or dinner gossip about students and their families), it is equally unethical, though not illegal, to withhold information from other professionals who need that information to work effectively and responsibly.

The Code of Ethics of the National Education Association, adopted by the 1975 Representative Assembly, states that "Educators ... shall not disclose information about students obtained in the course of professional service ... unless the disclosure serves a *compelling professional purpose* or is required by law" (Section 8, Principle 1, italics the authors'). Needed are some guidelines which would help us identify "compelling professional purpose." In parent conferencing, the NEA Code must be translated into those decisions which become our responsibility because they are not stipulated by administrative rulings or laws.

It would be simple if all we needed to do was advise: "Don't write down anything said by a parent or discuss what they said. Put your records in language so bland that it does not communicate and, therefore, cannot be challenged." Obviously, such advice would not serve professional purposes because:

1. Knowledge of a student's home life and parental influences often is a vital part of the information needed to teach that student effectively (*Chapter 3*). Not to share essential information with others who also work with the student or who subsequently will work with him/her could handicap the student.

2. Students benefit when teachers have information from those who previously worked with the student's family or who know family members from a different perspective. That information can be valuable in establishing and achieving appropriate conference objectives.

3. Follow-up work becomes haphazard or impossible unless agreements and responsibilities are recorded.

4. Objective evaluation of work is not possible unless records of progress are kept.

5. Professional growth demands consultations with other professionals about those aspects of our work we question. This involves talking about what we did and might do in response to what we have learned about a student and the family.

6. The growth of junior professionals (beginning teachers and student teachers) demands we share our expertise with them in order that they become more proficient in conferencing. This means talking with them about what they have learned through conferences, records, or from other sources. It also may mean sharing information and examples from our own work.

It is clear then that the ethics of confidentiality do *not* demand that we *not* disclose what we know about those we serve, but require us to share the information with certain precautions and under certain specified circumstances with those who need it to render quality service.

In addition to laws or administrative rulings, there are guidelines and precautions which govern ethical use of information.

GUIDELINES FOR SHARING INFORMATION

1. *Within Our Own School*

a. To do a quality job, we seek knowledge acquired in the past by other professionals (previous teachers of the student, specialists, guidance people, including the nurse and administrators) so we know *parents* as thoroughly and as quickly as possible.

b. To know the *student* better, we get information from other school staff to clarify or validate our observations so that reports to and work with the parents are based on sound information.

c. To increase our own competence, we discuss information about students or their families when we consult with others on the staff (other teachers with expertise in the field, supervisors, consultants, specialists and administrators).

d. To increase the competence of others on our staff, we share information with them.

2. *With Individuals or Agencies Outside Our Own School*

a. We share information with specified individuals or agencies when directed to do so, *in writing*, by parents or legal guardians or by the students themselves if they are over 18 years of age.

b. If we consult about our own professional work or development with a person not on our own school staff, we share pertinent information with them without disclosing the personal identity of the student or family.

PRECAUTIONS IN SHARING INFORMATION

1. *Within Our Own School*

a. Intraschool sharing of information does *not* require written consent. However, as an ethical procedure, when we have information which we believe needs to be shared with others in our school, we determine whether or not parents should be asked for their consent. If parents know the purpose of our information sharing, it is likely that they will give their permission.

Examples:

"David's next teacher should know this. It will help him/her to understand the situation and work successfully right from the start. Do you agree?"

"This is something that our principal ought to know, so the necessary arrangements can be made. I'd like to talk with him/her about it."

"If I discuss this with the school nurse, she may be able to come up with a suggestion of how best to handle the situation."

"I'm not sure what would be best. If you don't mind, I'd like to talk it over with _____, who may have a different perspective, and that could be helpful."

b. Professionals in allied fields are increasingly respectful of protecting rights to privacy among family members, and ask for consent for sharing information gained from one with another. Teachers also need to express this respect for confidentiality. We cannot assume that what a mother says is to be divulged to the father or vice versa or what parents and students say may be divulged to each other unless this is checked out and consent is received.

Examples:

"Do you want your mother to know about it?" would be a question to ask a student when there is a choice.

"I know you would prefer your parents not know this, but I have the responsibility to them. Would you prefer to tell them and how will I know that you have?" which demonstrates respect for that student's right to privacy.

"If your husband (wife) comes in for a conference, do you want him (her) to know this?" would be a question to ask one parent regarding information to be given to the other.

Recorded information is available to either parent, upon request, regardless of the desires of the other parent or the student.

c. Clerical staff, school aides and volunteers *must be specifically trained in the ethics and standards of conduct necessary for professionally handling information.* Our own modeling will assist them to acquire a professional stance with information they have gathered as part of their work with students and their families. Without training, no one should have access to information which potentially could be an invasion of privacy.

d. Even in our own school we should not talk with or show anything to anyone who is not directly involved with the student's education unless it is for purposes of professional development.

In deciding with whom to share information, we need to be assured that the other person will adhere to the same ethical code that we do. If we give information about a student or a family to the student's next teacher or we consult with the school social worker, the nurse or anyone else, we must know that colleague will regard the information as confidential. To insure this, we need to reiterate cautions about confidentiality.

2. *Outside Our School*

a. Requests for information about students from any individual, institution or agency must include legal written permission for release of information, in order that we may respond. This is a long standing practice.

b. There is, as yet, no definite legal ruling regarding the length of time for which a signed permission for release of information is valid (practices vary among institutions and practitioners). We ask parents, legal guardians or students over 18 years of age for specific directions each school year as to whether a previously signed consent for release of information to a particular resource should be honored.

c. If we do not have written permission for release of information, we do not respond to phone calls requesting information about a student or a family, no matter how the person identifies him/herself, nor de we even admit we know of the existence of that student or family. We politely request, "Please write me a note, giving me your name and what you need to know and enclose signed permission for the release of the information you wish or have whoever is legally responsible contact me directly. Then I'll be glad to talk with you."

The law does permit disclosure without consent in situations where we have "good faith reasons" to believe an emergency exists in which someone's life or health is at stake.

d. We are cautious if someone from another school within the district or the district office calls. We check whether or not the information requested requires a signed consent for release of information, take the name and phone number and *return* the call, to make sure that we are speaking with the person working at that school or district office and it is someone who has a legitimate right to receive the information.

WORKING NOTES

Our own working notes, not shared with others, are not part of the student's official record. We are extremely careful to keep those notes in a place which insures their confidentiality with no possibility for their being inadvertently seen by others. We need to be aware that any person could quickly glance at a page of notes on our desk or that a student can easily learn that in a certain unlocked drawer is a folder with interesting information.

We put notes made during one conference away before we greet the next parent, and we put away *all* notes even if we leave the room for just a few moments between conferences. When not in use, we lock up all notes or secure them in some other way.

ADDITIONAL PRECAUTIONS

1. We know that one way to protect the privacy of students and their families is *not* to have information about them. This is one reason we caution against listening to information which does not directly help us to educate the student (*Chapter 21*).

2. Whenever the names of students or their families are not essential (as they usually are not when we consult with others for our own or their professional growth), we disguise identities as much as possible.

In summary, we learn only what is important to know for working effectively. We share this information only when required to by law, to increase the probability of extending quality service to the student or to further our own or other's professional development. While following the laws of our district and the community, we lean over backwards to protect the rights to privacy of those whom we serve.

Section V   SPECIAL PROBLEMS

20. BEING THE BEARER OF BAD TIDINGS
     How do I communicate unwelcome information? 77

21. A LISTENING POST FOR PARENTS
     To be or not to be? 80

22. ADVICE SEEKING PARENTS
     Should I tell them what to do? 81

23. RELUCTANT PARENTS
     How do I get them to a conference?. 83

24. THE ANGRY, VERBALLY ABUSIVE PARENT
     What do I do when they're mad?. 85

25. THE UNSCHEDULED, "DROP IN" CONFERENCE
     Do you have a minute? 87

26. PREMATURE CLOSURES
     Let's settle it quickly 90

BEING THE BEARER OF BAD TIDINGS

Effective communication demands that we give parents valid reports about their child no matter how difficult or painful we feel that information may be for us to deliver or for parents to hear.

Being the bearer of bad tidings is difficult for most of us because the training we received as children, reinforced by experience, was: "Don't say unpleasant things." "Don't hurt other people's feelings. It's not polite." Thus we are torn between being polite and being professionally responsible. Since it is hard to speak about things we suspect may be difficult for someone else to hear, we often find excuses not to say clearly, or even say at all, what we know needs to be said. This is as true for other professionals as it is for educators.

Pediatricians can have difficulty in telling parents that their newborn is a defective baby. Some have asked a nurse to break the news, others have asked for test after test, even when the evidence was as conclusive as current techniques could make it. What kept them from telling the parent, since the facts were there and could not be altered? It is our guess that those physicians, like all of us, have a hard time being the bearer of bad tidings.

It is understandable that we would rather deal with pleasant than unpleasant topics. It is our professional responsibility, however, to communicate well considered educational observations and conclusions to parents. That is what, in part, we are paid to do. Avoiding, hedging, postponing, thinking we have insufficient evidence does not further the work of educating students.

Unfortunately, we sometimes use nonproductive techniques that protect us from the discomfort of being a bearer of bad tidings and become victims of the "I don't want to deal with it" syndrome. We may hope that someone else will tell "it," that the parents will find out about "it" through other channels, or that if we wait long enough, "it" will go away. As a last resort, we can hope that the parents will move out of the district and we won't have to tell them.

Five techniques commonly used to avoid being the bearer of bad tidings are:

1. *The Conspiracy of Silence.*
Time after time, as if by tacit agreement, a subject is not brought up although both parents and teacher know the problem exists.

Example: The teacher and Charlotte's parents, who are high achieving leaders in the community, focus on things to talk about in the conference other than the girl's obvious lack of academic progress. Even after a number of years of evidence that she struggles to barely keep up with her classmate and her interests are not in school work, her nonachievement is not discussed. Conference talk resolves around the private secondary schools or the high powered college the parents attended, with the unspoken implication that Charlotte, of course, will follow her parents' footsteps, a future the teacher feels to be highly unlikely but avoids discussing.

2. *Participants Behaving as if the Conference Were a Social Situation.*
Conference time is expended with exchanges of recipes, discussion of the PTA, school outings, the awful state of education, the world, youth, etc. Small talk, playing the "ain't-it-awful" game and social conversations may, for the moment, help both teacher and parent feel reprieved. Expending time this way however, is simply a dodge to avoid the difficult task at hand.

3. *Postponing.*
Again and again one is tempted to believe that there is insufficient evidence to discuss a difficult situation. There certainly needs to be ample evidence for validation of what we consider to be facts. In education, however, as in any other "people profession," there are few certainties. Being a professional involves taking the risk of using *available*, not hoped-for or conclusive, evidence in arriving at conclusions and making decisions. If there is new information, later perceptions and decisions can be revised. That too, is professionally sound.

It doesn't help when Charlotte's parents are told, "She's just a late bloomer," and precious time is expended on examples such as Albert Einstein who is said to have not learned to read until he was quite old or other equally nontypical examples.

While some children do take more time than others to come into their own, when the teacher feels that the student isn't catching on, a statement about the child's achievement needs to be made. The qualifying, "I'm not yet concerned because _____" or "I've begun to be concerned because _____," followed by a recommendation as to what might be a productive course to follow, needs to be communicated.

4. *Hedging, Using Unclear Language or "Euphe-nothings."*
A statement clothed in unclear verbiage or *almost* saying what needs to be said, *isn't* saying it. We need to say it straight, and through our use of check-back (see *Chapter 10*) insure that the parents understood what we told them.

5. *The Blame-Game.*
Educators, at times, do not place responsibility where it belongs and take refuge in, "I'm not to blame. *He* is, *you* or *they* are." The child's intellectual endowment, health, a previous teacher, school system or the state of the community or world also can be blamed. Allocation of responsibility is often followed by: "Because it's not my fault, don't expect me to do anything. I'm not the one who is responsible. You (or they) should do something."

A common cry from teachers is: "What can I do with a child who comes from such an environment?" followed by: "If only the family would _____" which is an understandable wish for a teacher who is at her/his wit's end. But even if the family *did*, the results might not be as far reaching as desired. Besides, there could not be a miraculous change by tomorrow morning when the teacher has to deal with that student in the classroom. Consequently, a school strategy for change or a school and home plan must be determined, agreed to, implemented, monitored and evaluated. (See *Chapter 4*)

It may help us avoid these nonproductive techniques and face the pain of communicating unwelcome information if we separate the difficulty of saying something from the difficulty of the situation that exists. *It is the existence of a problem which hurts, not the naming of that problem.*

Life is often difficult and even unjust. There is illness; there are unfulfilled hopes and dreams; kids are in trouble. These things hurt bitterly. On the other hand, once a difficult situation has been brought out into the open, has been communicated and examined, people can begin to deal with it. When people know they are ill, they can learn to plan constructively. If parents know that their child has been truant, failing in school or using drugs, they can begin to deal with those facts. There may be an initial shock, but there is often a feeling of respect and even gratitude toward the person who "had enough faith in and respect for me to tell me." Most parents often feel that harm was done when they were not given facts when those facts became apparent and consider it a "gift" to be with someone who cares enough to deal honestly with one of their most basic concerns, the growth and development of their child.

Using the techniques described in this book enables us to put difficult messages into words in a way that is potentially growth evoking rather than crushing.

A LISTENING POST FOR PARENTS

Teachers need to be good listeners, but they also need to know when *not to listen.*

Some parents bring "stories" ostensibly as "information." Their motives may range from joy in sharing something with an understanding adult who also is involved with their child, to loneliness, to inexperience or unwillingness to be selective in sharing information, to gossip. The wise teacher soon learns not to be used as a listening post for information which does not directly relate to working with the student.

Without this discrimination, we waste hours listening to trivia, being polite or hopeful that something useful may turn up. We need to develop toughness in making decisions about what legitimately belongs in the category of *useful* information.

Not being willing to listen can be difficult. Conflicts arise between being gracious, therefore listening, and being professional, therefore not listening, to a parent. We have been taught that it is not polite to shut people off. We also know we should not be misused.

Inexperienced teachers can be flattered by seemingly having won the trust of a parent, but this soon palls. It takes professional discrimination to determine when to engage in constructive and professional listening or polite but professional turning off.

Two situations where we need to say clearly, "I'm not the one for you to talk to about this" are:

(1) When we suspect that the parent would be better served by telling his/her story to a different professional. In this case, we need to tell the parent courteously but firmly, "I think it would be better if you talked with _____ (the principal, counselor, nurse or other professional in the school), who can be more helpful to you than I could possibly be."

(2) When a parent's disclosures of personal situations may become a cause for later discomfort or lead to conflicts regarding confidentiality. (See *Chapter 19*). Permitting such revelations will diminish rather than build trust and rapport between home and school, just as we might never again wish to see someone who witnessed us in a very painful or embarrassing situation, who knows something that we really don't wish known.

It is professional to stop inappropriate revelations by, "I can see your heart is full. But I think it is best if I didn't know about this. I have to be quite objective working with your child and I find that I cannot be if I hear too much that isn't directly concerned with what I need to know about him/her."

While "caring listening" is an essential trait for every teacher, knowing when *not* to listen also is a professional skill which is an important aspect of our competence.

Should I tell them what to do?

ADVICE SEEKING PARENTS

Teachers often are knowledgeable and available professionals with whom parents can talk about problems in child-rearing. Also, teachers are partners in concern about a particular child's functioning and learning. Consequently, many parents ask their child's teacher for advice.

The counsel requested includes suggestions regarding appropriate reading materials, how to best help youngsters with homework, limit TV, get the child to bed on time, what might be done to increase their child's ability to play productively with peers, plus a host of other concerns. Frequently, teachers are competent to give the requested information and welcome such requests as appropriate joint ventures on which to work, because a successful response could result in the student's improved functioning at school.

Teachers also need to be aware that they may become just one more person in a long line of advice-givers for the parent. Often people don't need more advice. They need help to put into operation the advice they already have been given. Articles, books, physicians, ministers, neighbors, relatives, teachers, have offered advice. Many parents have had more advice than they know what to do with. For some who don't intend to *do* anything, seeking additional advice can be a way of avoiding action. They are merely "advice shopping."

Teachers can be helpful to advice seeking parents when they:

1. *Determine what the parent has already tried and how it worked.*

"What have you tried so far? How did it work out?" are questions that identify whether or not parents have thought through the situation and intend to direct action towards a solution of the problem.

2. *Teach parents specific skills which they could use to improve students functioning.* (See Chapter 4)

3. *Give parents emotional support.*

Because they feel close to their child's teachers and because teachers share parental concerns about children, parents may ask for advice about their children when they are feeling in need of emotional support for themselves.

Teachers can be supportive of the efforts and strengths in the parent and of the parent's feelings. "I know how hard you have worked and I hear your despair." "In spite of all your efforts, it still hasn't worked out and I know you're terribly disappointed." "I can see how difficult it must be for you to _____." Indications that someone recognizes one's feelings can be most helpful.

4. *Clarify questions or concerns.*

It is within the skill and competence of many teachers to help parents clarify their *real* concern, when, as so often happens, this is not clear. Is it the child's behavior or achievement? Or is it that mother wants father to *do* something. Is it the need to have someone to talk to, or is father really wanting to be more effective in "getting Johnny to do something?" Does mother want the teacher to know that her marriage is on the rocks so the teacher can be aware of special stresses on the student, or does the mother want help with her marital problem and hopes that the teacher will hear her need and suggest appropriate counsel?

5. *Determine those situations where a teacher cannot be helpful to parents.*

Teachers are not trained to help a parent cope more effectively with problems such as family illness, a marriage breakup, a spouse's habits, personality, or response to the children, interfering relatives, the parent's own hang-ups. When such problems are brought to teachers, a referral should be made to the appropriate person at school. We might say: "I'm sorry, I'm not the one to help you with this. You need to talk with _____ who is more able to suggest where you might get the help you need."

Referrals to any out-of-school resource are highly complicated and require specialized processes and action, not within the usual preparation of teachers. School administrators or guidance personnel, as part of their training, learn about appropriate referrals in the community, practitioners in a particular field or agency, as well as requirements for admissions, waiting lists, fees, etc. Persons with this information have the best chance to match the parent in need of a referral with the available resource.

Teachers also *cannot* be helpful when there is a non-child-centered motive for the parent's requests. Some mothers, tied to the home and child-rearing, have few adults with whom to talk, especially adults who will listen empathically. Those parents may express an unmet need by taking their concerns to teachers. Teachers can be almost victimized, because, in our society, it is rare for parents to have someone to talk to who is interested and involved in their children and their problems. (See *Chapter 21*)

Whenever we feel inadequate or uncomfortable with a parent's request for counsel, it is important that we give ourselves the right *not* to respond. We might say, "I hear you are troubled (or you have important questions), but I'm not the best one to help you. You might talk to _____. If you wish, I'll help you arrange an appointment."

Teachers fulfill their educational role when they help parents by:

1. Giving information or advice in their area of competence.

2. Teaching parents some child-rearing skills which will result in improved home and school functioning.

3. Being supportive of parents' strengths, efforts and feelings.

4. Clarifying problems.

5. Referring parents, when the situation is beyond the teacher's skills or comfort, to appropriate school staff for counsel or for referral to an appropriate community resource.

Only experience can guide us in knowing what is a real plea to have someone hear pain, or a real request for help which we feel competent to give, in contrast to parents' avoiding action by shopping for advice, sympathy or a willing ear. Mistakes in judgment will be made, as they are inevitably made by other professionals.

If we limit help to our areas of training and competence and for every other request resolutely refer the parent to an appropriate person within the school, we will stay on safe and productive professional grounds.

RELUCTANT PARENTS

"I really need to talk with that mother. If only I could get her in for a conference. Isn't she interested in her child at all?"

That mother might well be interested. Her way of expressing interest, however, may be different from the teacher's expectations and may not include close contact with the school. Almost all parents are keenly interested in the education of their children even when their reluctance to come to school for a conference gives the impression that they are not.

Some parents do not enter easily into a working relationship with their children's teachers. Their reasons may be based in cultural differences or previous life experiences including experiences with schools, weariness, overwork, illness or lack of awareness of the value of home-school collaboration. Some of those parents can become engaged in a more cooperative relation if, and only if, *teachers reach out to them.*

POSITIVE MESSAGES

Schools, in the past, mainly made contact with parents when there was a problem. As a result, many parents have developed a chain reaction: "The teacher wants to see me, that means my child has problems." Problems can trigger avoidance.

When teachers make contact with parents to share desired information and positive experiences, parents learn to look forward to seeing their child's teacher. When parents get occasional notes or phone calls from teachers about the effort their child is making, something new that has been learned (including social, athletic and artistic growth), a personality trait in the child which is desirable or appealing, they will develop an attitude toward the school different from that of parents who never receive a message which would help them feel good about themselves or their children.

It is impossible to overemphasize the power of occasional positive messages either verbal or written such as:

"Jenny wrote such a good story today we put it up on the board for all the children to read."

"Bill really sat quietly and listened today. He surely is growing in his ability to pay attention when he is in a larger group."

"Gretchen has worked hard all week on learning new words. Soon she'll know them so well she'll want to take her book home to read to you."

"Rob looks so great in his new outfit."

"Manuel learned to divide today. He's so happy and proud he beams with pleasure."

"I'm so pleased for Beatrice. She has made a really nice friend in Felicia, and she shows that life is just different when you have a friend."

With some high powered, high achieving parents, who are too busy or self involved to maintain contact with the school, positive messages often are an effective way to direct needed constructive attention to their child.

INVITATION TO VISIT

A cordial written or phoned invitation to visit the classroom in order to observe students at work may be a less threatening initial contact than a face-to-face conference. The group conference (*Chapter 1*) also provides an easy beginning.

PHONE CONFERENCES

Parents who cannot come to school or who consistently break appointments, may be helped to become less reluctant by a phone conference. (*Chapter 18*) Eventually, after several phone conversations, they may be willing to come to school.

No matter what we do, not every parent's inability or reluctance to actively cooperate with the school will dissipate. Nevertheless, the joy parents experience when they hear about their child's successful attempts to learn and grow is something to which they are entitled. At the very least, the parent will have a chance to develop more pleasant associations with the school and often a we-are-caring-for-your-child-together atmosphere is created, which, in time of stress or crisis, can pay off handsomely.

84

THE ANGRY, VERBALLY ABUSIVE PARENT

To meet with a verbally abusive parent is a trying, unpleasant experience which arouses feelings in us that range from fear or helplessness to anger.

Strong negative parental feelings may be expressed in many ways: verbal outbursts towards teachers, nonsupport of bond elections or school programs, nonparticipation, and criticism of administrators, teachers or school board members. Verbal outbursts directed towards us in a conference, however, present a difficult situation with which to deal.

As professionals, we have the additional problem of awareness of our own feelings: what is going on within us when confronted by an angry parent. Are we feeling anger, resentment, indignation, fear? Acknowledging that the parent is angry, but not necessarily with us, will ameliorate some stress.

Anger has been defined as a response to a *felt* (not necessarily actual) assault. What seems to us to be unreasonable anger on the part of a parent may be a reaction to years of having felt assaulted in many different ways. The incident which triggered the parent's outburst may be only a peg on which a lot of stored-up anger is hung.

Using effective techniques to respond to the parent will give us a feeling of professional strength.

While we may, at times, express ourselves strongly, we need to make every effort not to act angry even though, being human, we may be boiling inside. We do not do our best thinking under strong emotions. Consequently, we should err on the side of caution rather than doing something we will regret later. To accept abuse from parents, however, will accomplish nothing that will benefit the student, even in those cases when the shortcomings of the educational system or of the situation arouse justifiable parental displeasure.

When verbal anger is encountered, there are four stress reducing techniques which can be used alone or in combination. These are not listed in order of effectiveness, but are alternatives from which to choose.

1. *Listening Without Saying Anything.*

When no response to outbursts is made, sometimes parents will stop, collect themselves, apologize, and move to more productive communication.

2. *Acknowledging the Parent's Anger.*

Sometimes parents stop their outbursts when confronted by a calm statement describing what they are doing:

> "I hear that you are really angry."
> "I don't understand what you're saying. Only that you're angry."

"Well, one thing is sure. You know how to tell someone you're angry."

"You must have stored-up those feelings a long time for them to come out so strongly." (To which one parent replied, "For 42 years I've been mad at teachers." This interchange ended in laughter.)

If the anger is justified, we acknowledge it:

"I don't blame you for feeling that way. Let me tell you what happened and (if appropriate) what I propose to do to make amends."

"I made a mistake."

When parental anger expressed to us should be directed towards the school system or another social or political entity, and if social or political action might result in positive changes, we respond professionally by, "Many of us at school feel strongly about that situation and we're working to have it changed." If indicated, we add: "Here's what you could do to help," then direct the parent towards positive action.

3. *Telling the Parent How We Feel Without Becoming Emotional.*

"I feel uncomfortable when you raise your voice like that."

"I know you're angry, but bawling me out doesn't help me to think or even want to listen."

4. *Stopping the Conference.*

"I don't think it's going to be productive to talk today. We need to talk about _____, but we both need to be calm enough to think and willing to listen to each other."

"You are very angry today. I don't think it will be helpful if we continue."

"I really don't want to talk when you're so angry."

After a statement suggesting termination of the conference, we add: "Let's make another appointment for a time when we can be productive together."

If nothing else is accomplished by terminating the conference, we eliminate emotional wear and tear. In addition, it may save the parent from later feeling guilty or uncomfortable as a result of the outburst. At times, the suggestion to terminate the conference may snap the parent out of a tirade and enable him/her to participate productively.

One parent recounts an adroit teacher's handling of a potentially tense situation in a completely spontaneous way. The mother was upset about what she considered an unreasonable rule at her child's school. She went to the school, in her words, "ready to do battle." When she approached the teacher, whom she had not previously met, the teacher said, "Oh, you are Kelly's mother. I'm so glad to meet you. I've rarely had a cuter and brighter kid in my room. I enjoy her immensely and I hope you know what a treasure you have." The mother gulped and decided to "forget" about her complaint. Her additional comment was, "If teachers only knew what a positive comment can achieve, they'd start with one no matter what the issue is."

In summary, to avoid destructive interaction with an angry parent, we examine our own feelings and work to maintain professional composure and dignity. We acknowledge the parent's anger without accepting undeserved responsibility for it and we have available a repertoire of responses to use in times of stress.

Do you have a minute?

THE UNSCHEDULED DROP IN CONFERENCE

The following letter appeared in the Los Angeles Times.

Dear Abby:

I am a high school principal who has had it up to here with the thoughtless parents who just pop in at their convenience for a special conference.

Will you please ask parents who want to discuss a problem concerning their child to phone for an appointment or write a note? Other professionals do not accept walk-in conferences except in cases of emergency. Last week I had 16 walk-in meetings with parents! My time is scheduled, and I just can't see all these people who want to see me when it suits them.

Had It

Dear Had It:

You aren't the only one with this problem. Many teachers have complained too. I hope this helps.

Abby

We're sorry that Abby did not respond, "It takes two to tango."

While in an emergency we take a minute to exchange small bits of information or to respond to the first overture of a reluctant parent (see *Chapter 23*), for any other communication we *graciously* inform parents that a drop-in conference will not be satisfying to either of us and set a time for meeting.

At best, unscheduled conferences are a nuisance, as "Had It" points out. At worst, they short-change students and parents because we have not had time to prepare for a mutually satisfying interaction. We may also feel such conferences to be an imposition, and being imposed on disposes few of us to be at our best.

We need to raise the question of why so many parents drop in for conferences. Our hunch is that it is because our talking to parents without appointments gives them the impression that it is all right to do so. As a result, parents do not learn that it is *not* all right to drop in and that they should make appointments to see school professionals just as they do with other professionals. We will change this situation only when we are consistent in insisting that, with few exceptions, conferences are "by appointment only."

When a parent drops in with a request for information that cannot be handled in a brief encounter, we courteously ask the parent to tell us the essence of what (s)he wishes to talk about. Then, we follow with, "Let's set a time to talk about it," or "Fine, I'll be free at _____ and we can talk then if that's convenient." Some parents will counter with, "But I only wanted to know _____." In order not to be maneuvered into a potentially unsatisfactory situation, we steadfastly maintain, "I'm sorry that I am not available now. Let's set a time when we can sit down and talk comfortably."

Drop-in exchanges are acceptable if they involve giving or receiving small bits of information. Those brief encounters occur:

1. *As follow-up to previous communication.*

Examples:

Parent: Is George finishing his work now?
Teacher: Very much so. Thank you for your help.

Teacher: How is Muriel feeling about her homework?
Parent: She really likes having a choice as to when it's TV time and when it's homework time.

2. *To exchange information or give a cue to something important.*

Examples:

Teacher: Has Harold told you about the new science project? He seems really turned on by it.
Parent: Oh yes. He doesn't stop talking about it.

Teacher: Ask Manuel about the story he wrote today. It was great and I think he'd be pleased if he got a chance to tell you about it.
Parent: I will. Thanks for letting me know.

Parent: Jenny wasn't feeling too well this morning. I wasn't sure if she just didn't sleep well or whether she's coming down with something. Would you please watch her and call me if I should come and pick her up?
Teacher: I will. Thanks for letting me know.

3. *To make a conference appointment.*

A request for a conference can become a drop in conference if the teacher does not insist on scheduling a later unhurried time.

Example:

Teacher: I would like to talk to you about Danny's handling of frustrations. When would be a convenient time for you to come in?
Parent: Oh, is something wrong? Want my husband to come too?

Teacher: It would be great if he could come. I want to tell you what we've started to do to help Danny and see whether we can come up with some ideas you might also try at home.

Parent: Oh, what kinds of ideas?

Teacher: Let's make an appointment to talk about it when neither of us is rushed and when Danny's dad can be here too. There is no crisis—next week or the week after will be just fine.

There are times when teacher, parents, and child benefit from frequent short conferences. For those parents, we can schedule frequent 5 to 15 minute appointments and eliminate the drop-in habit.

As an additional precaution, schools can inform parents at meetings and through bulletins that teachers and other staff are always available by *appointment*. However, if teachers continue to hold conferences with parents who have not made appointments, no amount of informing parents what they *should* do will eliminate the problem. Those same parents are accustomed to making appointments with other professionals, a practice which gives them the opportunity to review charts or prepare whatever is necessary. To render quality educational service, teachers have the same professional obligation.

So, we resist the temptation to "do it now and get it over with." We make appointments so our thought-through preparation and procedures will help parents to appreciate that the wait was well worth it.

Let's settle it quickly.

PREMATURE CLOSURES

As soon as a problem has been identified, some parents seek closure with "What shall we do about it?"

Teachers often are tempted to come up with a quick solution even when the professional task is to understand the situation as fully as possible. Out of that understanding will come a working hypothesis that leads to plans with reasonable probability of success. These plans need not be perfect nor can they be. They can be revised after they are put into effect and correcting information becomes apparent.

For example, should a student have behavior problems, the things that either home or school "should do" depend on knowledge about the youngster, the situation in which the misbehavior occurs and what the people who work with that youngster are willing and able to do. In one situation, it might be best for either the teacher or the principal to say to the student, "If you can't behave in a way that shows you are grown-up enough to be in school, you must go home." In a different situation, this action would be inappropriate because the mother would make going home rewarding by letting the culprit bake cookies or watch TV all day. Suspension also will not work if the parent is unable to provide the essential home supervision. In such cases, an alternative solution needs to be devised which would be more appropriate.

Successful plans don't come from quick ready-mix recipes, but grow out of thoughtful deliberation and discussion that identifies important factors in the situation. Productive plans usually are developed cooperatively, have the strength of support of both family and school, and yield dividends that are far beyond the returns of any quick solution. Therefore, let us beware of that "let's settle it quickly" panacea.

Section VI   LOGISTICS

27. THE TIME, THE PLACE AND THE SETTING 92
   Where and when?

THE TIME, THE PLACE AND THE SETTING

The same warm, welcoming and personal atmosphere that we like to find in the office of physicians, lawyers or any of the helping professionals should be in the parent conference. Neither the teacher, who is giving a professional service, nor the parent, whose taxes are paying for it, deserves less.

THE SETTING

A well appointed office is not necessary. It is, however, important to have reasonable privacy, a place where the teacher is comfortable and feels "in charge of self and situation" and a surface where samples of student work can be laid out for viewing. A desk between teacher and parent can be perceived as a barrier and when there is only one adult sized chair in the room, it is best for all adults to use low chairs.

A "Do Not Disturb" sign on the classroom door is useful to avoid the possibility of students wandering in to look for jackets, books, lunch pails or whatever. Students can be taught what the sign means and to respect the message. The sign also cautions other parents or colleagues not to interrupt.

When conferencing with a number of parents in a row, some teachers have found it useful to post a schedule on the door so that parents have a "set" that they are one of many who will be seen that day and won't expect a leisurely, open-ended time.

Some schools, which have pupil-free periods or days set aside for parent conferences, use areas such as the gym or cafeteria to meet. A feeling of privacy is achieved by separating areas with potted plants, screens and whatever else is at hand. Coffee and cookies can be provided by the PTA and translators can be available for non-English speaking parents. Some teachers prefer this environment to classrooms.

THE SCHEDULE

Our conference schedule needs to reflect 1) our own preferences, 2) the availability of parents, 3) the anticipated time demands of the conference, and 4) special time provided by our school district.

1. *Our Own Preferences.*

To be effective, we need to be physically, intellectually and emotionally at our best. Therefore, we need to take into consideration our ability to tolerate shifts of focus, fatigue points and other personal or professional commitments.

a. *When to schedule conferences.*

For after school conferences, we usually need at least 15 minutes to recover from our teaching day, refresh ourselves, collect our thoughts, and organize materials we will use in the conference. An appointment immediately after dismissal of students will likely find us frazzled, keep parents waiting and result in frustration and dissatisfaction.

Some teachers and parents prefer early morning appointments. Others find that to be an interference with preparation for a day of work. Occasionally, noon conferences can be scheduled, but time constraints and work demands just before and after lunch can make this a not-so-desirable time. After school, preferably with early dismissal of students, or days set aside for conferencing by the school district, are usually more satisfactory for both teachers and parents.

b. *The number of conferences in a day.*

We need to determine how many conferences we can conduct before they melt into a blur and we lose hoped for gains from the communication. At some point, all of us experience overload, our intellectual fuses blow and we cease to function well. Most of us are not able to perform optimally beyond three to four successive conferences without an intervening time block to digest information and impressions. For that reason, a full day of conferencing may not be the best use of time.

c. *The time between conferences*

We also need to estimate the time between conferences that it takes us to shift gears from a discussion of one student to the next one. We may need a few moments to collect our thoughts, record important information and decisions from the conference just concluded, focus on the objective for the next conference and gather supporting materials for it. Parents are understandably uncomfortable when confronted by a breathless, "now let me think," over-scheduled teacher, and that teacher may not be comfortably in charge.

2. *Parental Preferences.*

Some parents are able to leave work early or are permitted to come in late to attend a school conference. Others can make arrangements with their employers to make up lost time. Some conferences are scheduled late in the afternoon or in the evening for parents who cannot come to school at any other time.

3. *The Time Needed to Accomplish the Conference Objectives.*

A half hour usually is sufficient for a well planned routine conference. For other conferences, we need to anticipate our and the parent's ability to get right down to business without sacrificing personal comfort and satisfaction, or the possibility of hitting emotional snags or complex problems which will take more than a half hour to identify and discuss.

The following generalizations may be useful:

Most problem solving conferences need more than half an hour.

The more people involved in a conference, the more time will be needed for each to participate fully.

Conferences with new parents may take longer than conferences with parents we already know.

Taking more time to discuss potentially painful topics may not be useful. Indeed, to be brief (without being hurried or abrupt), precise and problem-solving oriented may be enabling to parents in that it conveys our belief that they are capable of dealing with the subject at hand. Over-explanations and over-solicitations may be an indication of our own discomfort rather than a response to the need of the parent. (See *Chapter 20*)

When we can anticipate that a conference may be difficult or time consuming, it is best to schedule it when it is not followed by another conference or by teaching responsibility. In this way, the parent does not feel rushed or "bumped" by the discomfort of another parent or students waiting. Also, we can devote our energy to the situation that requires it without withholding to have some energy available for our next task.

When a routine conference turns out to be one which needs additional time, it is best to schedule another conference rather than run overtime.

4. *Conference Time Provided by School Districts.*

Many districts periodically schedule pupil-free periods or days for reporting conferences so teachers have time without teaching duties. Although special conference time is desirable and a step in the right direction, sometimes hoped for gains are not fully realized. Teachers can be overwhelmed by seeing too many parents in a row on these pupil free days. Conferences melt into each other. The time allotted for each conference may be too short and keeping to a schedule is too hectic a pace for either parent or teacher to feel satisfied. Many teachers use the provided-for time, but lessen the conference density by seeing some parents at other times.

Each of us must decide what we are able and willing to physically and emotionally accommodate in terms of the time when we are available to parents, the density of a conference schedule, and the availability of parents. Usually, stretching a point to make ourselves available (without becoming exhausted or exploited) yields rich dividends in home-school cooperation, collaboration and student learning.

Setting, schedules and time are relatively easy to arrange in advance and contribute a great deal towards removal of the irritation that will emerge if those aspects are not considered. Taking care of them leaves us free to devote our professional skill and energy to the substance of the conference and the communicative interactions that accomplish our objectives.

Section VII SAMPLE FORMS

Invitation to Group Conference. 96

Invitation to Reporting Conference 97

Written Summaries. 98

Follow-up Letters 100

Weekly Note. 102

Student Questionnaires. 103

INVITATION TO GROUP CONFERENCE

Dear Parents:

We are looking forward to becoming acquainted with you and letting you know what a good start our class has made as well as telling you about what we will work to accomplish this year.

On Tuesday, September 29, at 7:30 p.m., we will have a 15 minute get-acquainted coffee time so you can meet the parents of your child's classmates. Promptly at 7:45 p.m. we will tell you about the program for the year and suggest ways you can help your child increase his/her learning. We will conclude the meeting by 8:45 p.m.

This will not be a time when we discuss your individual child. Just as soon as we are well acquainted with him/her we will set a time to meet with each of you individually.

To make sure we answer your general concerns at this first meeting, please jot down your questions or special interests on the tear-off below and return it to school by your child.

Remember the date, *Tuesday, September 29, 7:30 p.m.* We'll look forward to seeing you.

_____
Teacher(s)

I will ____ will not ____ be able to attend the meeting on Tuesday, September 29.

I would like the meeting to include information about _____

_____

_____

Child _____   Parent _____

INVITATION TO REPORTING CONFERENCE

Dear _____,

    I am looking forward to meeting with you to report your child's progress on _____ at _____ o'clock. Should this time not be satisfactory for you, please indicate more convenient alternatives on the form below. I will make every effort to meet one of them.

    So our conference will be focused on your interests, questions or concerns, as well as on your child's general growth and achievement, will you please indicate any areas which you want me to especially emphasize.

                              _____
                              Teacher

_____The appointment on _____ is satisfactory.
                      day   time
_____I am unable to meet at the time you suggest.

Could we meet on _____ or _____
                 day   time   day   time
I am especially interested in:

_____

_____

_____

Child's name _____ Parent _____

Diane R.   Nov. 13

1. No academic concerns, doing well.

2. Work on downgrading self and others.
   At School
      a. We'll identify kinder comments. She'll
        practice them with me and then others.
      b. I'll watch + keep daily record on card.
      c. She'll take card home on Fri.
      d. If she's mad, she'll tell me or write it down
        but <u>won</u>'t say anything to others for awhile.
   At home, you will:
      a. Check card each Friday + give approval
        for good marks, do nothing for poor marks.
      b. Plan something special when she has 4 out
        of 5 good days.
      c. Make (model) positive comments to her and
        others in the family.

3. We'll meet in a month to see how its going.

98

Richard M.   June 1

1. Richard is pleasant and cooperative. Works hard. Wants to please and succeed.

2. Difficulties are in reading and math.

3. To avoid summer loss again in reading,

    a. have him read to you 5 min. each day. I'll send a list of books.

    b. have him play word games I showed you.

    c. have him do some work alone, but supervise..

    d. continue the special help program he now has.

4. Practice number facts with a household account book. Record items, cost and total them each week. On trip he will keep mileage and gas acct.

5. You'll spend time together on household chores he likes, with lots of conversation.

6. For "bookkeeping" and chores he'll earn privileges you agree on like staying up later.

7. We'll plan extra reading and math help next year at school.

99

FOLLOW-UP LETTER

November 1

Mr. and Mrs. John Doe
10 Any Street
City, California   Re: Adam

Dear Mr. and Mrs. Doe:

As promised, I'm summarizing the main points of our conference yesterday when we discussed Adam's achievements and what he needs to do to improve his skills and feeling of competence.

We agreed that I will talk with Adam and set up the following homework program.

1. He will have work sheets for spelling and handwriting. I will check his work each week and, on a chart, record how well he is doing.

2. For math, Adam will make his own multiplication flashcards. He will be responsible for learning the facts assigned to him.

3. He will read aloud to you for five minutes each night. You will ask him questions about what he has read in the way I showed you at school. I will send a book that is at the right level of difficulty so he can be responsible for understanding what he has read.

4. He will record the beginning and ending time of his homework each evening (approximately half an hour) and be responsible for bringing that record to school once a week.

5. I will help him chart his progress at school so he will have tangible evidence of his academic growth.

After our conference, I talked with Adam about his reading, writing and math, and ways he could grow with help from you, from me, and through his own efforts. He said he was anxious to accomplish more.

Your help in eliminating distractions while he is working plus listening to him read each evening and asking him about what he has read, will not only be of great assistance to his learning, but convince him of your faith in his ability and your willingness to work with him.

Please call me if you have any questions. Otherwise, as agreed, I will call you in two weeks to check how things are going at home and report how Adam is progressing in school.

This could be the beginning of an important growth spurt for Adam. Thank you for your assistance.

Sincerely,

_____

Teacher

100

FOLLOW-UP LETTER

January 1

Mr. and Mrs. John Doe
100 Any Street
USA City, California

Re: Sarah

Dear Mr. and Mrs. Doe:

As agreed, I am summarizing our conference yesterday. Sarah, as far as we can tell, does not have any difficulties with learning because of perceptual problems or because she hasn't matured enough to succeed with reading or writing. She seems bright, and when she pays attention she grasps instructions quickly. The problem is that, often, she does not pay attention and, therefore, she is not learning at the rate we expect.

You and I decided that both at school and at home we would make sure that Sarah listens and follows directions. We also agreed that we would give ourselves six weeks to see how successful we are and then get together for a review and further planning.

At school we will do the following:

1. Have her follow directions more promptly without arguing or asking if she may do something else first. I will start by holding her responsible for coming to instructional groups without delay.

2. I will give her a note with "happy face" or a comment "good job" for every period she does well. She may take those notes home to share with you.

3. Before she starts her work I will ask her to repeat the directions given to the group and praise her when she knows what she is to do and then does it.

At home, you will work on eliminating Sarah's complaining about what you serve for dinner.

1. You will talk with her and explain that you don't like to be nagged about what you serve and that you will help her learn not to nag.

2. Every night that Sarah eats her dinner without complaining, she will get a mark on her chart. When she has four marks she may choose the food for the next meal. If she "forgets" and complains you will say nothing. She will not get her good mark and, therefore, her choosing what to have for dinner will be postponed.

We talked about your finding her very tense and saying she is hungry when you pick her up from school. You agreed to have a snack with you. Even if her "ravenousness" isn't due to lack of food, that may help reduce her tension and make the ride home more enjoyable for everyone. If she is pleasant, you will comment positively on something about her which also will help her feel better about herself.

I think our plans will work, but be sure to let me know if you run into any difficulties. I, also, will feel free to call you if I have anything special to report.

Thank you for your openness and cooperation. I enjoyed talking with you and feel very encouraged about our working together to help Sarah attend to those tasks which both you and I know she can do and will feel proud of herself when she masters them.

Sincerely,

_____

Teacher

101

WEEKLY NOTE

Dear_____,

Again this week, Steve and I can report that he has finished all his follow-up work in reading and language. When we consider that those are not his favorite subjects, he is to be commended for following through on the plan the three of us made at our conference. In addition, I can see steady improvement in the quality of his thinking and the legibility of his writing.

I'm sure that with his continued effort we can soon forget our concerns about his language skills.

_____

Teacher

STUDENT QUESTIONNAIRE

(Younger students)

Teacher interview with student prior to parent conference:

1. What do you enjoy doing at school?
2. What do you least enjoy doing at school?
3. Who are your best friends?
4. With which new friends would you like to work or play?
5. What would you like to do or learn about that you haven't had a chance to do yet?
6. What do you want your parents to be sure to know about you at school?
7. Help me find your work you want them to see.

STUDENT QUESTIONNAIRE

(Older students)

Date _____

Name _____

Teacher's name _____

Student Self-Assessment

Period covered:

From _____ To _____

I enjoyed _____ most, because _____

I enjoyed _____ so-so, because _____

I enjoyed _____ least, because _____

My easiest subject is _____

My hardest subject is _____

I'm best friends in school with _____

I want my mom and/or dad to know about _____

I want to be present when my teacher and my mom and/or dad conference about me _____.

I don't want to be present in the conference _____.